What makes this anthology so engaging is that it offers insightful reflections on Paula's many contributions to Native literary and Gender Studies (and chili cooking) in many forms and from several generations: essays, poems, fiction, an interview, a funeral eulogy, and wonderful photos from Paula's mentors, colleagues, and students. To borrow Paula's own phrase, this is a tasty and nutritious full "story pot."

—KENNETH ROEMER
Co-Editor, *The Cambridge Companion to Native American Literature*

⟶ᔕᐦᓓ⟵

Like the woman it honors, this volume brims with humorous tales and bold resistance. The personal stories will first break your heart and then remake it—returning both a stronger and more compassionate vessel. The authors invoke the "multiversity" of Paula Gunn Allen's Indigenous and feminist teachings, tracing its influence on Native scholarship and on their own becoming as writers, scholars, and activists.

—KIMBERLY BLAESER
author of *Apprenticed to Justice*,
Wisconsin Poet Laureate 2015-16

Weaving the Legacy

From beyond time,
beyond oak trees and bright clear water flow,
she was given the work of weaving the strands
of her body, her pain, her vision
into creation, and the gift of having created,
to disappear.

—excerpt from the poem "Grandmother"
by Paula Gunn Allen from *Life is a Fatal Disease*

WEAVING THE LEGACY

Remembering Paula Gunn Allen

EDITED BY

Stephanie A. Sellers
and Menoukha R. Case

West End Press | Albuquerque

First edition

Paperback ISBN 978-0-9970353-1-5

West End Press | P.O. Box 27334 | Albuquerque, New Mexico 87125

For book information, see our website at www.westendpress.org

Library of Congress Cataloging in Publication Data is available online.

Book design and composition by Lila Romero

Cover photograph courtesy of Carolyn Dunn

Decorative border on cover: Plate XX[d]. Acoma manta illustration: Pueblo Indian Embroidery, H.P. Mera, 1943. Archives, Museum of Indian Arts & Culture, Laboratory of Anthropology, Santa Fe.

TABLE OF CONTENTS

CONTENTS

CONTENTS

DEDICATION

Old Hopi Home
Kristina Bitsue

Patricia Clark Smith

February 14, 1943–July 11, 2010
Professor Emerita, University of New Mexico

Stephanie A. Sellers

With profound respect and no less love, I dedicate this work to the teacher and writer Patricia Clark Smith (Irish, French Canadian, and Micmac Indian). She is the Elder of this issue who nourished and mentored Paula, the mentor we are lauding and remembering; therefore, it is she who has also touched each one of us.

Patricia Clark Smith advised Paula Gunn Allen's dissertation at the University of New Mexico and was one of Paula's close friends. That dissertation later became the groundbreaking work in Native American women's studies, *The Sacred Hoop* (1986) that has now shaped generations of scholars and empowered innumerable women. Since Paula was my dissertation advisor, I was the recipient of Pat's teachings as well, as her wisdom passed from Paula to me.

Pat responded to the Call for Papers for this volume by contacting me. Since then, we have been growing our friendship, and I feel so privileged to have received mentoring from such an outstanding scholar, poet, and woman.

On July 13, 2010 I came to town to my campus office and was hoping to find an email from Pat. Less than a week before she had sent her final comments on the essay I wrote that appears in this volume. Instead of an email from Pat, however, I found an obituary from the Association for the Study of American Indian Literatures saying she had died over the weekend.

I was shocked by the depth of my own grief at losing Pat and this is, to me, the testament of how deeply her friendship touched me. I am only one among so many who feel this way.

This dedication is just one of the many ways that I want to say "Thank You" to Patricia Clark Smith.

Here is an excerpt from her obituary sent by email from a member of the English department at University of New Mexico on July 15, 2010:

Patricia (Pat) Clark Smith died peacefully at Women's Hospital in Albuquerque Sunday evening, July 11. She had been admitted four days earlier and died of successive organ failure. She was surrounded at death by her husband John Crawford, her two sons Joshua and Caleb, members of her extended family, and her friends.

Patricia was born on Valentine's Day in Holyoke, Massachusetts in 1943 and while she was later renowned as an accomplished scholar, poet, and teacher, she always stayed close to her working-class Irish, French Canadian, and Micmac Indian roots. She attended Smith College as a scholarship student, graduating with a B.A. in 1964, and Yale University from 1964 to 1970, when she was awarded a Ph.D. in English. She taught English at University of New Mexico for thirty-two years, from 1971 to 2003. Early in her career at UNM she also taught at schools connected to several Navajo Indian reservations (Ramah and Sinosti) in New Mexico with a new mentor, pioneering New Mexico early childhood teacher Lenore Wolfe. Pat married teacher and small press publisher (West End Press) John Crawford in 1987.

One of her early Ph.D. students, Laguna Pueblo author Paula Gunn Allen, published a revised version of her doctoral dissertation as *The Sacred Hoop*, a groundbreaking approach to feminist studies in Native American literature, in 1986. Among Patricia's companions throughout this period were Native American writers Joy Harjo, Leslie Marmon Silko, Simon Ortiz and Luci Tapahonso. She published the first book of her own poems, *Talking to the Land*, in 1979.

Those who have known her deeply—and there are many—have praised Patricia's generosity, her ability to bring out the best in others, and her gift of encouragement. She has started many a young writer or scholar on his or her career. Her advocacy for women scholars, multicultural writers, and especially Native American students has moved the teaching profession powerfully in this region. She has also befriended many people she recognizes as her own kind—waitresses, nurses in hospitals, receptionists, and clerks in stores.

PUBLISHED BOOKS

Western Literature in a World Context. Editor, with Paul Davis, Gary Harrison, David Johnson, and John Crawford. St. Martin's Press, New York, 1995.

As Long as the Rivers Flow: The Stories of Nine Native Americans. With Paula Gunn Allen. Scholastic, New York, 1996.

On the Trail of Elder Brother: Glous'gap Stories of the Micmac Indians. With Michael B. RunningWolf. Persea Books, New York, 2000.

Weetamoo: Heart of the Pocassets. Scholastic, New York, 2003.

PUBLISHED POETRY COLLECTIONS

Talking to the Land. Blue Moon Press. Tucson, 1979.

Changing Your Story. West End Press. Albuquerque, 1991.

Patricia Clark Smith
February 14, 1943–July 11, 2010

Portrait by permission from Family

Survival Letter to Paula
for Paula Gunn Allen

Patricia Clark Smith

You again   beautiful vaudevillian
homing back from up north   from playing the Micmac
reading those poems you make up someway
out of grace   raw meat

Head thrown back on a cushion
brush back your black hair:

I'm goin' good for an Indian girl
these last two months
I've slept with one Asian
one black, and a blind guy

the twist of your mouth
I laugh
choke Coors clean across the room

and tell you about my Navajo students
Diné ridin high while I drove their schoolbus
air conditioner out and wanting a beer
with red rock and roll coming off the tape deck

Res-ervaTION of ED-ucation
49ing songs, they knew all the words:
Doo ya shoodi da
biligåana
always something slightly skewed
in white man white man
biligåana

--You get that one Pat? they call from up back,
--Yeah, sure. (Sweat, downshifting fast,
highballing down La Bajada Hill.)
That time I made songs in my head
me Snowwhite
me drive Rosered

Good drinking good talk
poems and men
and playing the old games. Someday we say
two breeds on a quest
we will seek out the Wise Old Anglo Man.
We will know him.
Whole reservoirs
great gates of water
gleam in the tail of his wise white eyes.
He is drunk on vision
mad with Old Charter
blowing smoke from a chimney in four directions

Grandfather we will say teach us how to see
Daughters he will say my sweet sloe plums
laying his hands somewhere about us
mumbling of mirrors
lasers electricity

Laguna lady my darkblood friend
better drunkards you say than watered fools

Tonight I dream you show up at my door
summer night like this
wind out of the west and Scorpio rising
Antares starheart pulse red as rimrock
cicada earthchild down by the river
nightchant sifting down from cottonwoods

and beyond this valley your mesas waiting
where gods, the woman ones are walking
Tse-che-naku Changing Woman Grandmother Spider
fullbodied wideminded they stroll the high ground

they want us strong, Paula
with a clean welcome
they take us on
laughing

(Albuquerque, 1976)

INTRODUCTION

Anasazi Window
Kristina Bitsue

PREFACE

Paula Gunn Allen As I Knew Her

Maurice Kenny

Mountain Song

Let me sprinkle pollen
over your head
tell / the tales that hold the rocks to life
I
will walk nobly to Bush Mountain
lost to the redstone gates of dawn.
The treacherous potholes are drunk on clouds.
The enemy has many wiles.

Paula Gunn Allen [1]

A peach, a handful of peaches falling to the ground, a bushel of peaches. This is how I remember best Paula Gunn Allen, not as the famed erudite scholar, the poet, the novelist, the critic. Not that she should not be remembered as such, but

---

1 First published in *From the Center*, Strawberry Press, 198.

decidedly she deserves that remembrance; the woman worked hard and earned that right. Obviously this wonder woman deserves whatever accolade for her strong talents and praise for the difficult and important work she accomplished in Native Studies and her own successful creative pursuits. I remember her best as the friend, the woman, the colleague picking peaches from her tree on land where she lived near the Albuquerque city limits.

We stood together beneath the hot sun, sweat on our chins . . . it was blistering. We laughed biting into the delectably sweet fruit, its juices sliding down the chin, hands sticky from the nectar. She asked if I had ever before accomplished such a feat . . . picking ripened fruit under a roasting sun. Well, yes and no, I replied that I had picked wild sour cherries from my sister's fruit tree in her back yard. Once while picking, I sat on a stout tree limb, fighting off blackbirds who were as eager as I to pick this fruit. She laughed. "Well, we're doing that now except birds are smarter than us as they are cool in the shade and we are turning black in the sun." We laughed heartily. She was correct once again.

For the next few days of steamy western desert blaze we baked pies and froze them; canned peaches for the cellar; ate peach shortcake for supper desserts and packed away large baskets to take to the roadside as gifts for whatever family in an auto might be coming up Paula's road. There is little doubt she had not a self-ish bone in her frame. She gave much away to the needy: a place to sleep on her floor for a poet passing through, a cold glass of water to a person hiking the highway, or she would drive granny or grandpa to the store on a Saturday morning for their meager pro-visions . . . regardless of what she herself might have in the larder or refrigerator, let alone what was in her purse. She heeded to the old rule of share.

In a comic way, I have always thought of her as the "peach" lady, which gives a little tug at the strings.

When did we and how did we meet those years back? Once more a strong memory eases up from the deep well of remembrance. I had met three young Native artists through a San Francisco newspaper, three students who were directors of a particular radio show on KPOO, "Red Voices." These kids were advertising for Native people to come and be on the show to sing, tell tribal stories or contemporary situations, read poetry, plays, or music, or speak of memoirs, whatever. Their names were Randy Burns, Barbara Cameron (sadly, now deceased), and Sharol Graves. The two women were students at Mills College in Oakland, Sharol a dance major/potter, Barbara a writer who eventually earned a job at *Mother Jones*, while Randy was a student at San Francisco State and at that moment was taking courses in Native American law and had known Paula Gunn Allen, who was chair of Native Studies, from another lit class.

He mentioned to Dr. Allen that he had recently met a world famous Native poet. She was curious . . . a Native poet from back East! I'd supposed she asked for reference and name, but not recognizing Randy's newly found poet, shuffled the thought off and dismissed the eager student as teachers are wont. Randy persisted that this poet had been published in an anthology of "third world" writers. It was entitled "From the Belly of the Shark," edited by Walter Lowenfels, a famous poet/editor. The poet had been published many times in *Akwesasne Notes*, a national magazine published at Akwesasne, a Mohawk reservation in Northern New York, near the St. Lawrence River. Paula recognized the magazine and suggested to Randy she would be interested in meeting his new friend. "Ask him to pass by my office," which I did almost immediately, and we took off in a flight of words.

At the time I was co-editor of *Contact/11 Poetry Magazine* and *Contact/11 Publications*, named after William Carlos Williams' magazine *Contact* and was about to print Native American poets in a new venue named Strawberry Press. Paula, Lance Hendon, and Wendy Rose were early poets to be printed by Strawberry Press. Paula's choice for the title of her slim collection was *A Cannon Between My Knees* . . . a fiery title. It sold out. A few years later she announces that she had regrets in the title, that it made her seem or sound as if she had gone to war as a hard feminist. I soothed her fears and Paula wrote and carried onto the road to greater days and greater works, but the slender collection of poems sent her into the national poetry scene.

Once she admitted her thought was to change her name back to Francis . . . her father's family name. We upped and downed about the change. Finally she was convinced that the literary world had grabbed onto Gunn and Allen and would not shake it off. It would take time possibly, years maybe, to re-invent herself with the name of Francis. Paula gave it considerable consideration and came to realize I was correct. Time is always precious and a fleeting commodity. She kept Gunn Allen and whispered Francis to the night.

Back to our friendship, and speaking of food, I cannot continue writing this memoir of Paula without telling the world of her cooking expertise and absolute joy in setting a place she might prepare for a visiting guest. (Though not without a smile and guffaw once the diner had tasted her delight on the table.) The one dish I remember clearer than any other was her fabulous chili. I do not recall her naming the dish con carne (though it was such) but only as chili. I had lived in Mexico City for two and one half years before meeting Paula. I had eaten most of the more famous foods served in this grand but poor country. I had enjoyed everything . . . some things I did not believe I would ever have a taste for such as ceviche (raw fish), goat meat, flesh hanging in the market covered in flies, chicken hearts wrapped in a hot tortilla, and other such things.

In Merida, the Yucatan, I bit into a tiny green chili . . . encouraged by a young waiter who stood back and observed my attention to the food on the served platter. This was many years past when I was visiting Willard Motley, the novelist, in his "pink house" on the hill overlooking Mexico City. Merida: covered by flowers, dense with human smiles, bending with waiter responses to service, and ready to leave the diner's presence for a huge laugh. I kept pushing the green thing away. The waiter moved closer and pushed it towards my fork. There were four or five on a tiny tray. "Por favor, señor, please try the chili. Muy dulce." Trembling, I raised it to my lips where it got no further than the teeth. I near screamed in horrific pain. The waiter had gathered a few other waiters and they in chorus raised the roof in laughter.

Which returns my thought to Paula's chili. I had always known it to be made of chopped beef, otherwise known as hamburger. Not Paula's contents. She went to the butcher, not a supermarket, and purchased any number of pounds of raw beef. Fine! She also bought fresh chilies. I was asked to leave the kitchen as she wanted no one to learn her particular recipe. I obliged and went to stroll in the yard. When her supper was prepared, finished and stewing, she called. I was to sit at a table with a large napkin and she served a bowl of steaming chili. Red Hot! Hot as a Laguna sun might bake a rock. I was overjoyed, smiled broadly, picked up the fork and dug in the dish. In seconds I rushed to the bathroom while Paula turned every color on the palette in laughter at my monkey-like shenanigans. She had forgotten to place a pitcher of ice water at the dining table. I died! My tongue sautéed over the flames. I perspired for days thereafter. She'd cooked my goose, so to speak.

As time went on she thrilled at telling the story about the Mohawk poet who couldn't take the southwestern food fare. Wherever she is at this moment, I'm sure she is giggling . . . like the waiters in Merida.

Under all conditions, Paula Gunn Allen was an excellent, succulent cook, and took pride in her astute knowledge of cooking and definitely in the fare of the southwest and Indian countries. As an adult you might wonder what it was like to have been born near her apron . . . If she wore one, which is doubtful. She loved to eat. She loved to cook, even when it was tough to allow herself the proper time to prepare for an invited and special guest.

What Paula was able to accomplish in her short life was amazing: the famed husbands, the wreath of children, the teaching, her traveling from state to state as she was wont to do, and changing colleges at a whim, sometimes mid-semester. Once she left New Mexico for another school in Colorado with the idea that I might take over her schedule, for which that particular university was to pay me a slight 500 dollars (which I refused even though I was out of work). Her thought was more generous than lawless. She rambled off as fast as her wagon would get her up that mountain slope to the new college.

Not only did she possess finely tuned brains, a sharp and sometimes caustic tongue, and a twinkling but beautiful brown eye, she could out-think you every time you thought your feet were fresh from bed on the cold floor. Her wit and intelligence had it thought out and mastered before your big toe hit that floor.

Tell Paula there was a pow wow down the road 500 miles and she was there before you thanked her for the invitation to travel along in the van, even if it might be over for the weekend by the time she hauled into the designated parking spot with a car full of hapless family or reckless students grieving over the fact that the pow wow was the next weekend or had been the one before. She smiled, lit up a cigarette to say, "well, it probably wasn't going to be a good one anyway." It was nothing gained but she knew it wasn't really anything lost. She'd toss her dark hair, smile profoundly and kiss air. My belief is that she loved running and driving around with the western breeze between her teeth. She did love the west . . . especially New Mexico.

The woman was brilliant! Her poems and fiction were good. She loved poetry, short story, and the novel, and the real, such as the neighbor down the arroyo, the student in the class she was teaching, her beloved father and her adored grandmother. Paula thoroughly enjoyed, respected and wished always to perpetuate the customs and culture of her/the Native people of home country and wherever else in her America. Once in New York City at an MLA meeting she proudly announced that the reason there was so much great art and literature coming from the southwest was due to the fact the Native People of that country stood on the earth, their earth. Her belief was right. Paula was there before most of us got to that path.

Her knowledge was more than extensive, studied, digested . . . it was of a quality unbeknown to most scholars of her age, service, persuasion and definite need. She lived every day her "specialty." She grew as the light of morning grew into the falling of sunset. Her mind was not only collective, but open, sorted things out, dismissed if need be, collected if of value, yet there was a laugh, a joke, sometimes a tear or a regret. Humility was there but the verbal prankster was not far behind the stage curtain. She could cut as well as paste. She could slice through words as though she sliced a peach for cobbler. She knew the answer before most of us knew the question.

She adored talking . . . just plain old gabbing, gossiping. Writers thrive on gossip, neighborhoods' whispers whether of the prairie or city. She filed these bits of gossip away to be used once an important tale needed flushing, filling out. The neighborhood was always there and revered for the tales. She was well aware that teaching was through storytelling. It was the best method and she refused to turn down an eye to life as it lay before, beneath and around her. She did stand on her earth . . . and firmly her feet were planted on rock and cactus of home. It made little difference where she was, whether teaching at UCLA, making a speech in Chicago, reading poems in San Francisco, birthing a child in Albuquerque, or dancing a Round Dance wherever there was drum and rattle music for the people and she called it her home.

The last time I was with Paula was in New York City, I was renting in Brooklyn, the famed Heights close to the great bridge where many a famous writer lived, and actors such as Normal Mailer and Truman Capote and Robert Redford. It was a small brownstone apartment on the third floor where we had cock roached, ghosts roaming our hallway, a landlord . . . Mr. Weizman . . . who often forgot to collect the rent or ignore it because he knew we might be starving poets; not far from State Street where stood the bar Wounded Knee and many Mohawk men who were the iron workers, some who in years past had died at the construction of the mammoth icon, the Brooklyn Bridge built by father and son Roebling. The winds only know whether Paula Gunn Allen will be remembered for having spent many different weekends in that brownstone apartment, and particularly when the last time she slept over there was a great assemblage of American writers of all colors and concerns in New York City.

Paula arrived with the very fine poet Judy Grahn, who was allergic to cigarette smoke. Poor Paula and I were forced to stand at the open window of the shaft blowing our cigarette smoke to the world, laughing at each other for being such stupid smokers. It was a tiny bathroom. The world was changing. Poets and storytellers and playwrights of color were at last recognized for the genius they possessed. That night Audre Lorde stood before the assembled writers and shouted to the world, "We are taking our language back." And that is exactly what Paula Gunn Allen did for the remaining days of her fruitful life and work. We gave each other a little hug, a smile, and went off to the big event knowing that a great thing was to be accomplished over that eventful weekend.

Snap, crackle, pop . . . Paula's language, thought, and movement of her critical ideals and creative discoveries and evaluations added to her final sentence on a certain subject . . . mainly life and pursuit and historical longevity of Native American culture. Ideas were thoroughly, deeply over time considered, but often sounding as though spit out on the second. Not true! Her brilliance would never have allowed such a travesty. She knew from memory, reality, definite study and simply opening her ears and listening, without doubt seeing with uncluttered sight. Her tongue could make summer breezes but also mash a fraudulent idea as a hammer a rock. Her tantalizing smile was infective, her disregard and anger everlasting, as a storm swipes away a fly with a snarl and blink of an eyelash. Her charm was always there hidden, often behind a smirk, in a joke or tease which obviously was her method of proving points and dismissing untruths for downright foolishness.

Years ago in North Beach, San Francisco, she and I were offered a reading in an old abandoned church. At the moment I do not recall which poetry reading series it was, but whatever it was, there we were, sitting on the stage; we were announced, and I rose to offer my poems. Paula was to introduce me . . . now I believed that I would soon by turn introduce her. Apparently we were not well known sufficiently to be introduced by the directors of the series. She stood, smiled at the audience, began to innumerate my publications and stated that I was half Mohawk and half Irish . . . she was not exactly sure which "testicle!" was which . . . naturally forgetting she was nearly as pale as my own flesh . . . she announces with a straight face. Historically the half-bloods were always suspect. Her eyes sparkled in humor. She possessed a wonderful sense of the ridiculous.

Paula and I had many great conversations over the years, some whimsical nearing stupidity and others deadly near the intensity of a grenade exploding on a battlefield of literature. We agreed that Leslie Marmon Silko was dominating modern fiction; Simon Ortiz was probably the head of the poet-pack. But allow me to clear the path for both Paula and myself. It is difficult if not wrong to attempt to evaluate the continuously enlarging numbers of Native writers popping up from the reservations . . . such as Jim Welch, Louise Erdrich, Anna Lee Walters, the late Ted Williams, Elizabeth Cook-Lynn, the grip in the fiction of Lorne Simon, the often humorous novels of Eric Gansworth; Peter Blue Cloud for his incredibly delicious antics of his trickster in stories and serious poems, not to suggest his coyote tales have less gold. Surely we cannot dismiss the glories and beauties and the sensitive veins in the poems of Joy Harjo, Duane Niatum, Mary TallMountain, often the brilliant short minimalist poems of Lance Henson, or the bite of the late Diane Burns who had the ginger and honesty of a bumblebee . . . or the great beauty and mastery of language that James Thomas Stevens has wrought from his pen . . . to offer only a few names.

Paula was almost always on the mark . . . of course she would change this idea and say, "I'm always on the mark" . . . such as telling me once that I probably used the word "blood" in the historical sense as much as Shakespeare. Now she was not saying, naturally, as well as Shakespeare. But she meant a compliment of dare. Also, when she further announced seriously the idea that I was probably the first contemporary Native poet/writer to emphasize sex as a theme, though often hidden in my poem and other writings. I did blush at this comment. She was astute, indeed. I hate to admit it but she was rarely wrong in her decisions. Allen the literary detective was always on the prowl with flashlight and pen. She made wrong decisions only in her husbands.

Her whip stung! Her rapier sliced . . . she was rarely wrong in her assumptions. Yet she gave not exactly tons of peaches, but gave this sweet fruit to many passers-by. And I must always remember the fridge was stacked with peach pie for whoever may knock on her door.

Paula Gunn Allen's words and language explode faster than the thought has time to borne. The peaches are seeded in my memory. Her flashing eyes and smart words are also canned for a later time on the shelf in my brain. Her time was brief. Now I regret this memory appears so short, as we had many years of friendship.

Introduction

Stephanie A. Sellers & Menoukha R. Case

You are welcomed to this anthology through Kristina Bitsue's image, "Old Hopi Home," and the first speaker is co-editor Stephanie A. Sellers, who dedicates this book to Paula Gunn Allen's (and Stephanie's) mentor Patricia Clark Smith. The heart of Paula's story was shared by many, and Pat captures that story well in her poem about Paula, titled "Survival Letter." Bitsue's image, "Anasazi Window," gives you a first glimpse of the interior of this book and beckons you inside its pages to listen to the stories.

A Mohawk Elder is the first voice to speak about Paula. Maurice Kenny's gorgeous Preface, that is spilling with peaches and burning chili-fire and the hot summer pavements of New York in the 1960s that roared the Native American Literary Renaissance to life among the voices of Audre Lorde and Paula Gunn Allen, invites us all to Paula's table to feed on a banquet of words. And when reading the words of the late Mohawk poet, we can be assured that we will be very well fed. Did we mention Maurice's favorite? Not red chili of the southwest, but the sweet red of the heart berry of his motherland in the northeast that speaks through seven decades of his poetry. Strawberries, always strawberries. Come and feast with us.

This anthology honors Paula Gunn Allen as a scholar, creative writer, and deeply engaged community member whose presence persists as a living legacy. Intrinsic to her life and career is a set of practices arising from a cohesive yet fluidly variable vision that has consistently stretched, broken, challenged, or escaped altogether the rules, bounds, and dominance of EuroAmerican colonial culture. Paula's vision and tenacity in adding an Indigenous voice to the classrooms and libraries of the Ivory Tower, and her insistence, through decades of publishing, teaching, and lecturing across the country, that the Indigenous experience be included, at long last, in the creation of American Indian Studies Departments, are central to her legacy. Yet this legacy exceeds even the relatively welcoming bounds of Indigenous oriented departments, as her work continues to find its way into Gender Studies, Cultural Studies, and Literary Criticism syllabi. Joining other Indigenous scholars and writers in accomplishing this monumental task, what she created is a road for Indigenous women to follow—a road where scholars and poets of any ethnicity can also find inspiration. She went up ahead and with her machete of words and wit chopped through the toughest barriers so future generations can follow an easier trail. This is why so many people revere her—witnessing Paula find her own voice helped us find ours.

Paula Gunn Allen's work pushes forward the kinds of academic queries that challenge race, class, sexuality, ability, and gender as oppressive cultural constructions. Her views on the Anglo-academic camp of the Second Wave feminist movement are well known: she was fooled by it for a while, as she says, but realized, as many Indigenous women eventually do, that we will never be included in that camp even when individual Anglo women are strong allies. This is readily acknowledged by many Anglo feminists today, but solutions to talk across the cultural divide are hard to come by. This is partly because, by its very nature, the

EuroAmerican version of western culture is radically antithetical to Indigenous worldviews and has embedded in its foundation a pervasive belief in white, male supremacy, no matter how diligently it is interrogated. Paula, along with both Anglo and non-Anglo women, did not allow this invisible supremacy to speak for the women's movements or women's empowerment, which they knew pre-dated (by thousands of years) even the so-called "First Waves" in many cultures around the world. The non-Native scholar, Sally Roesch Wagner, speaks directly to this issue in her work *Sisters in Spirit: Haudenosaunee (Iroquois) Influence on Early American Feminists* (Native Voices 2001).

Paula's work positioning women in Indigenous gynocratic social structures from antiquity received harsh criticism even from influential Indigenous academics, like Gerald Vizenor (Ojibwe), who made claims using white-feminist terminology to discount the ancient cultural stories and practices of Indigenous nations relating to gender. Ironically, the recent, definitive scholarship of Brenda J. Child (*Holding Our World Together: Ojibwe Women and the Survival of Community*, Penguin 2013) fully substantiates Paula's observations of women's primacy in some Indigenous nations made nearly thirty-years ago in *The Sacred Hoop* as they relate to the Ojibwe people. This is just one demonstration of how Paula's work bears out upon further scrutiny, and with the test of time, counters earlier criticism.

Paula's artistic and scholarly practices were not arbitrary, and the stretches, breaks, and escapes in literary structures and academic norms were not accidental. Rather, they arose from and are deeply rooted in Paula's understanding of Native gynocratic principles. Indeed, she has noted (in *The Sacred Hoop* and elsewhere) that if feminists were to study these principles, we could save ourselves the heartache and labor of reinventing the cultural wheel meant to centralize women, elders, and LGBT2-identifying individuals. This is because gynocratic principles express a paradigmatic understanding of the nature of reality that is radically different from the operative trajectory of EuroAmerican culture. While feminists struggle to dismantle a present that is already dysfunctional and scarily rolling towards absolute dystopia, Paula's work springs from the traditional egalitarian wisdom of many Indigenous cultures, taking a rooted stand in a past that is, in many ways, exactly where we claim we want to be: thus the appearance of rolling backwards. At times in Paula's work it appears she is going back into the past instead of forward into the future. However, the future is already here, as it has always been, and we must awaken from the nightmare of destruction that colonizers keep trying to make us believe is the only reality that can exist. Supremacy is nothing but a puppet show with lethal consequences performed by the colonizers and their converts; Indigenous realities continue unharmed. As Paula says, When evil takes over, the beauty is hidden away until it is safe to come out again.

Indeed, the very idea of backwards and forward is based on unquestioned accession—"the act by which one nation becomes party to an agreement already in force between other powers"—through the concept of linear time. Paula never acceded her nation's heritage, which includes the wisdom of cyclical timekeeping, to rules agreed on between "other powers." Her eyebrows would have raised at the joke of calling them powers. What kind of power can one ultimately steal by following recently-invented, delusional rules (tick tock, cha-ching) when your origins come from ancient cultural wisdom? Her work reaffirms, time and again, that Mother Earth sets the limits on the foolishness of modernity. Paula's legacy is the voice that reminds, re-directs, and offers new possibilities of coping with current struggles from a mindset of Indigenous cultural wholeness.

ANTHOLOGY AS STORY POT

In *Voice of the Turtle: American Indian Literature 1900-1970* (Ballantine Books 1994) Paula writes, "Any given narrative arises out of a vast constellation of stories, formal and informal, personal or 'high art,' and it is this all-encompassing matrix that provides a given work its apparently 'self-contained' meaning" (xi). She goes on to add that writers contribute to a "common story pot" (xii) when writing on specific themes, and this is indeed what we as editors have requested from writers and artists concerning the life and work of Paula Gunn Allen.

Recognized among many Indigenous cultures is the miraculous and unlikely pot—birch bark pots in which women boil water, woven cedar root pots and red-clay earthen pots in which women carry water, and so on. Not only useful, but also aesthetically satisfying and life-sustaining, these traditional vessels symbolize the story pot from which this anthology contributes a multiplicity of voices. Its weaving of the unexpected carries stories just as a pot carries water—to give life to the next generations.

The collection is therefore, first and foremost, a story pot of voices gathered from the many trails Paula walked—about Paula at times, but primarily about the struggles of Indigenous people negotiating identity, survival, joy, and the writer's life in the teeth of colonization. This book provides a straightforward catalogue of her professional life, but it is just as much a guide and teaching about the very worlds she touched, negotiated, and, in the end, transformed by her presence. Like her final brilliant work, *Pocahontas: Medicine Woman, Spy, Entrepreneur, Diplomat* (Harper-Collins 2004) that was nominated posthumously for the Pulitzer Prize, Paula provided not only a new lens for looking at history, biography, and cultures, but a template to re-understand human experiences.

The scholarly and creative works in this anthology are woven to carry Indigenous and non-Indigenous voices that reflect on-going scholarly discourse in Literary Studies, Gender Studies, and Native American Studies that carry on the legacy of Paula Gunn Allen. Their intellectual genesis is fleshed out and given an emotional dimension through personal stories of mentoring, through creative imagery, both written and visual. Together they carry forward Paula's teachings, her influence on her close mentees as well as distant readers, impacting the direction of contemporary teachers in the academy, and reaching countless generations stretching into the future.

Kristina Bitsue's poems and photographs throughout the anthology provide a creative thread drawing the binding of the work together with the voice of an Indigenous woman's stories and images of life—an important foil for the academic dialogue that, if not properly tended to, can become disembodied theory that lacks relevance to human experience. Bitsue's work keeps the anthology grounded in a human life, where all Indigenous scholarship eventually must claim a home. At any place in this collection, readers can dip into the pot and find works strong enough to begin important interrogations about what it means to be Indigenous, mixed blood, a woman, and/or a writer or artist—all woven together under the tutelage of a great storyteller and teacher whose legacy will outlive us all.

READING INDIGENOUS LITERATURES

Experiencing any work from an Indigenous writer, tribal collective, or filmmaker, warrants first a conversation about how to do so in an informed way that magnifies, rather than convolutes, that experience. Readers unfamiliar with Native literatures, cultures, and literary theory will benefit from the following brief lessons. Concepts like the story wheel or pot, cyclic time, relationship with the earth and ancestors, and Indigenous colonial experiences may be entirely new to many readers, and as your editors, we wish to expound on these fundamental concepts to aid the reading. Below are key considerations to keep in mind when reading an Indigenous work of art or scholarship that can only reveal a greater richness and truth from the works herewith.

COMMUNAL ETHICS

First of all, the oral and written works of Indigenous nations of the Americas cannot be understood in isolation since the very cultures themselves are reflections of the belief in communal ethics. This is the belief that every living being is in direct relationship with all-that-is and has an interdependent existence. We are all relatives, in other words, and are engaged in intimate reciprocal relationships that recognize the indwelling sanctity of every living being. Indigenous cultures of the Americas recognize this reality and express it through ritual, ceremony, socioeconomic practices, and in daily living. Therefore, stories themselves are members of the community—they are living realities and must be cared for by story keepers. Writing and recitation of stories feeds the story wheel or pot which then in turn feeds the whole community—an existence that is beyond this three-dimensional one.

CONCEPTS OF TIME

Second, in western culture time is understood and expressed in a linear form. Discrete moments in time are understood as past, present, or future, never all at once, and are therefore intrinsically disconnected. That is, events of the past are understood as "over" and fixed, therefore inaccessible and unalterable, and events of the future are understood as not yet formed and also inaccessible. But to most Indigenous nations, time is understood as events occurring in cycles—often conceptualized and described as "perennial now" or the "eternal now." This way of conceptualizing time recognizes that we are in constant relationship with our ancestors and with all future generations. It de-legitimizes the notion that cultural knowledge can be wholly lost "over time" because this knowledge continues to exist in previous cycles of time, and these cycles are still accessible. Storytellers play an important role in this accessibility to Time, and Time itself is like a being who possesses intelligence, memory, and spirit.

CENTRALITY OF LAND

Third, Indigenous relationship with the earth differs from what non-Natives often understand it to be. To westerners, culturally speaking, the earth is an "it"—a non-sentient, spiritless mass. Even folks who revere the earth for her beauty have deep cultural barriers in recognizing that, to many Native nations, she is Mother Earth. This term does not represent a recent invention by hippies or a cute endearment, but is an ancient term used by many Native nations to describe our very real relationship with the earth. A cultural value of communal ethics is behind this nomenclature (and is also present in most Native creation stories), but more than that, it is an acknowledgement that the earth too is a being who possesses intelligence, memory, and spirit.

The geographic locations in the Americas where Native nations originated determines specific features in their creation and teaching stories; in other words, Native stories are not about just any mountains, any rivers, or any landmark. Their stories are specific, for example, to a mountain where their people originated—like Mount Taylor or the Alleghenies—or a body of water like the Finger Lakes in New York State. When one considers the effects of Native removal from original homelands, it is easy to recognize the devastation to them when understanding that they are not connected broadly and simplistically to the earth, but to very specific places on the earth. Those places are relatives, literally.

Knowledge is in the land itself: " . . . combining . . . cyclic time with the centrality of the land, spiritual leader Ammoneta Sequoyah relays that if the valley is flooded his <u>knowledge</u> of medicine—and not just the medicinal plants themselves—will be lost. Mr. Sequoyah also notes that when he is buried this knowledge will be returned with him to the land . . . and . . . continue to be present [there] . . . for others to experience."[2]

COUNTERING ON-GOING COLONIZATION

Last, Indigenous colonial experiences are not over. As most Indigenous scholars rightly note, there is no such thing as "postcolonial"—not literature or history or culture. Settler boarding schools persisted into the 1960s and continuing cultural indoctrination and torture of Native children still haunts Indigenous nations. Intergenerational trauma is carried in the DNA and tribal memories of Native people living today, hence the Boarding School era itself still continues. The story in this anthology "Mestiza Nation: A Future History of my Tribe" speaks to this tragedy. Although methods have changed, land and children are still being stolen and displaced (see this National Public Radio report from October 25, 2011 "Native Foster Care: Lost Children, Shattered Families"), people are still being persecuted and murdered, and fresh graves are still being robbed by academics with research grants and professional "collectors" who sell goods on ebay.

Countering this, Indigenous cultures continue to co-opt settler culture and do what the Elders taught us to do—take the best of what the settlers have to offer and keep our traditions intact. Indeed, what is now understood as "traditional" looks quite

2 "Belonging to Land: Indigenous Knowledge Systems and the Natural World," 703, Vicki Grieves, Laurie Whitt, Waerete Norman and Mere Roberts, *The Oklahoma City University Law Review* Volume 26:1 and 2 Spring and Summer, 2001.

different from traditions of twenty to a hundred years ago—as it should! Culture is a living entity that must grow and change as the people do. Hence it is not at all uncommon to see young Native people today enjoying their iPods while wearing traditional dancing regalia! Communications from Standing Rock were not by smoke signals, but Digital Smoke Signals, as Myron Dewey calls his organization. He recorded events with drones and cleverly linked multiple cell accounts to bypass governmental or corporate efforts to cut off communication. Keen observation of the workings of things and savvy application of these observations for the good of the whole is a continuation of tradition, not assimilation.

LISTENING

The strategies and theoretical frameworks of the English tradition with which we are taught to interrogate literature do not work with Native stories, on the wheel or in the pot. Instead, they must be understood as rooted in spirit relationships with time, place, sacred geography, and a history that includes the future. We must understand those criteria from a Native point of view and have a reasonable understanding of some fundamental cultural beliefs in order to enter into the writing. Indigenous nations have been writing for millennia along with sustaining oral narratives of the community that are recited ritually at certain times of the year, so contemporary non-Native readers are witnessing and partaking of traditions that are ancient, not new, yet spoken in new tongues and reaching new ears. Readers are now part of the audience for this tradition and must learn how to be good listeners.

The creative and scholarly works in this anthology straddle divides between contemporary innovations and reliance on already established scholarship in the fields they address, and at the same time, they stand utterly on their own. It is not that writers in this collection don't engage traditional discourses—they do. However, we are concerned with the ways they intersect with, draw on, and overlap the tradition that is Paula Gunn Allen. Paula's work is a locus of tradition in and of itself, and her ground-breaking work in planting the field of Native American Studies is rooted in traditional values. Contributors to this anthology express their unique positions through their pieces and also converse with each other about interweaving perceptions and memories of the Grandmother. The conversation is not foreclosed or definitive; it is inclusive, sometimes of the fragment, sometimes fragmentary. Together all these pieces help us glimpse the field of beauty constituted by Paula.

We hope we have assisted readers in a deeper appreciation for the community of voices offered here in love, gratitude, and respect for Paula Gunn Allen. She gave so much to us all, and filled the story pot so full, that we will have much to discuss, argue about, and relish for decades to come.

THREADS OF THE WEAVING

Creating works that generate scholarly discourse—a deepening of historic and cultural knowledge and expansion on the human intellectual experience—is the hallmark of superb scholarship. The essays in this anthology directly engage Paula's literary and scholarly legacies through theoretical analysis and cross-discipline interrogations on themes such as Two-Spirit and Indigenous identities and Ecofeminism. However, they do so on Paula's terms as she framed the conversation over several decades of scholarship. That is, such discourse is not privileged, separated out, or excluded, but is present as part of the story pot.

Many of the artistic contributions of Indigenous women in this anthology speak to issues within the Native community—from boarding school traumas, to profound spiritual awakening, to their relationship with the land. The collection serves as a reflection of Paula's impact on Native American Studies as an academic discipline, but also continues her unique and complex scholarly trajectory by expanding on topics like Two-Spirit theory, Ecofeminism, and the struggles of Indigenous people in the academy. There are photographs of Paula's homeland, Laguna Pueblo, and the sacred geography of the American Southwest (a term she disdained), evocative images of earth and sky. There are also the reminiscing voices of friends recalling Paula's experiences as a young professor at University of California at Berkeley, thus creating a sketch of issues from that era for the historic record. Last, the eulogy from Paula's memorial service is included that testifies to the power of cross-national and mixed blood community-building Paula accomplished.

Time is the warp thread of Paula's simultaneous re-establishment of and extrapolations from her Native traditions. The woof is a colorful alteration of her gestures that created community, empowered individuals, and mentored scholars and artists, who in turn lend patterns to multiple disciplines in a collective weaving that astonishes with its creative beauty. Herewith are the voices of the anthology and the ways they build upon, intertwine, and reveal the greater issues of Paula's legacy.

SECTION I: "WE REMEMBER"

We are welcomed to this section with Bitsue's image "Old Beclabito" with its ancient formidable presence rising from the earth. Then the work of Barbara Alice Mann ("Paula Gunn Allen Retrospective") locates readers in the personal and professional experiences familiar to many Native American scholars and faculty in the Ivory Tower, what Mann wittily refers to as "yakademia." Her essay reveals what is still undeniably invisible to most in academia, the ongoing disciplinary and personal attacks on

Native peoples, as well as the solidarity that supported Paula's continuing struggle against historic exclusion. The thread of empowering individuals begins here, and Paula's gesture at the same time creates community, offering us the chance to reflect on how the two relate as part of communal ethics.

Janice Gould's essay "Dear Mentors: A Recollection," follows the thread of community, taking readers on a journey with the amazing teachers she encountered in the San Francisco Bay Area in the 1980s, like Cherríe Moraga, Gloria Anzaldúa, Ana Castillo, Nellie Wong, Merle Woo, Angela Davis, and June Jordan in addition to Indigenous poets and teachers like Chrystos, Patricia Clark Smith, Gerald Vizenor and, of course, Paula, who shaped her as a budding writer. From her initial contact with Paula, Gould notes that "knowing that Paula was a "sister" probably gave me the courage to ask her if she would read and critique some of my poems" and this opened the writing within Gould that led to her first publications.

In LeAnne Howe's work, readers get a rare glimpse of the deep affection Paula carried for her Jidoo (Lebanese grandfather) that brings to life the mixed-blood identity Paula so valued, the multicultural heritage that brought so much richness to her writing and her life. After reading Ursula LeGuin's 1989 full-page review of *Spider Woman's Granddaughters* in *The New York Times Book Review*, Howe recalls the excitement and challenges of the publishing world and provides a glimpse into one of the first readings of *SWG* at the Manhattan Theatre Club in NYC.

The threads of empowering individuals and creating community continue in the work of Gabrielle Welford & Elaine Jacobs ("Paula Gunn Allen and Mary TallMountain: Trickster, Jester, Clown"). Their co-authored selection offers a portrait of Allen that was magnetic and that fundamentally characterized her personality: the woman who laughs while she is fighting everything from racist academics to cancer. They do this through a compelling prose-poem that emphatically declares "your job is to have fun through it all."

Annette Van Dyke's essay "Paula Gunn Allen: Innovator of New Academic Disciplines" draws in the threads of Paula's contributions to Gender Studies in the very academy that in some ways besieged her. This essay offers clues as to what shaped the community-building practices described by Welford and Jacobs. Van Dyke states that Spirituality is central to Paula's work, "underpinning her championing of the restoration of gay and lesbian Native Americans to their rightful place."

Márgara Averbach's piece "'Bricolage' from the Other End of the Continent: My No Conversations with Paula Gunn Allen," discusses the powerful influence of Allen's work on her career life, her identity as a woman, and her writing—despite the fact that they never personally met. The essay significantly demonstrates the power of books and reading on women's lives—a value understood by every woman-centered press in the world—and how these tools can reach beyond time and space. Averbach offers a close discussion of Allen's primary works and how they influenced her throughout her journey, carrying us along a thread of literary criticism vital to Paula's multi, inter, or transdisciplinary weaving.

In Bitsue's poem "Grandmother's Children and Grandchildren," we feel the way family and community persist through time; we feel how knowledge lives in the land itself as Bitsue claims "And *shimasaani* (grandmother)/Even though I didn't say goodbye/ When I greet the sun/When I see the blue sky/And when I meet the Navajo moonlight/I know you will be there with me."

Remembering is not only fundamental in the continuation of culture. Remembering and recounting is what makes a person human, connected to the current community and its ancestors. It is also a strong component of counter-narratives that decolonize. The offerings in Section I engage readers in the important act of Remembering, both as witness and participant, as remembering is the hallmark of how Indigenous people, and First Nations on every continent, reinforce and sustain their identities.

SECTION II: "WE CARRY ON"

Bitsue's photograph titled "Vintage Wagon," is an apt metaphor for Section II of this collection. Though the wagon was obviously abandoned after years of usefulness to other people in another era, it continues as a reminder of that important past. However, the sheltering trees at its side with their lush leaves suggest that though there are new ways to carry the precious cargo of teachings that differ from the ways of the past, it is the same life that continues, that prevails. This is the heart of continuance of cultures in the face of colonizing intrusions.

We begin this section with Sellers's poem "Long Distance Gifts" published in *American Indian Culture and Research Journal*'s issue to honor Paula's life. The poem chronicles the relationship Sellers had with Paula when she was a doctoral student under Paula's direction. In the lines "from sea to shining sea/across purple mountains' majesty"—a play on the Woody Guthrie song "This Land is Your Land"—Sellers demonstrates one of the many strategies used by Indigenous people since 1492: centralize the Native experience by re-imagining settler words and concepts to de-colonize our experience.

This is similar to Deborah Miranda's work in this same section. Miranda's poem "For the White Lady Who Had Kokopelli's Statue

Removed From a State Park" is precisely the type of mischief-making that characterized Paula, while the poem demonstrates on-going issues of colonial authority over Indigenous cultural representations.

As Paula's research assistant at University of California at Los Angeles, Dunn takes readers on a poetic tour of her own personal and professional identity as an Indigenous woman and how Paula's work, mentorship, and friendship supported and shaped those experiences. Dunn writes poignantly of Indigenous Removal, the diasporas that continue to shape Native identity, and the role of education in survival and creating counter-narratives to colonial histories and ideologies in California and across the nations.

Jennifer Browdy's "Seeing Through Native Eyes: Paula Gunn Allen's Writing as Ritual and Prophecy" notes the legacy Allen left for future generations of activists and visionaries who wish to create a better human future. Browdy notes that Allen's works can be read as "visionary repositories of myth and ritual" and she chronicles the events of Allen's last months of life. Here we see all the threads—creating community, empowering individuals, mentoring scholars and artists (either directly or via printed words), who in turn lend patterns to Native Studies, Gender Studies, and Literary Studies, and beyond that: activism that persists through time, countering colonization and defending the land.

With the long-view of an elder, Bruchac recalls with affection and respect the young poet, Paula Gunn Allen's, publication in a land-mark anthology of Native American writers he edited thirty-three years ago. Words like cutting-edge, trickster, and literary critic flow throughout his remembrance of time spent with a woman who would become an icon in the discipline of Native American Studies, and in the hearts of the people who knew her.

Every drawing together is followed by pulling apart; every ending leads to a new beginning. Deborah Miranda's "Mestiza Nation: A Future History of My Tribe" is a poignant story about a motherless daughter that reflects the tragedy of forced assimilation through boarding schools, kidnapping of Native children by settler social agencies, and the effects of colonization on Native families. It is the story of the mixed bloods finding their home. In the end, the daughter is reclaimed by her people through the power and presence of Native storytelling tradition, the very tradition Paula fundamentally furthered in her work.

SECTION III: "WE CONTINUE TO WEAVE"

Bitsue's image "El Morro" hints at the indomitable presence of a culturally complex and enduring people that outlasts colonial attempts at total erasure because the descendants return to this place and remember what is left unspoken in the stones and earth—the spirit that nothing can destroy.

Paula is not gone; she continues to weave through the hands of those she lovingly mentored. In "Writing the Good Fight," Stephanie A. Sellers describes coming to terms with scholarly and personal exclusion in academia. The kinds of struggles both she and Allen experienced are placed in the context of how many non-Native academics claim to own Indigenous knowledge and control it through colonial means. Marginalized groups are urged to reinvent the story of academia toward a better, more inclusive one, and recognize that it was Allen who significantly contributed to incorporating Native American perspectives in academia along with distinguished Native scholars like Elizabeth Cook-Lynn and Simon Ortiz, among others.

Sandra Cox continues this discussion in her work "Some Ideas, like Paula's, Endure: The 'Essential' Allen, Two Spirit Identity

Politics and Native Literary Nationalism," as well as picking up the thread of Gender Studies carried into the weaving by Van Dyke. She takes issue with biting criticism of *The Sacred Hoop* by male Indigenous authors Craig Womack, Robert Warrior, and Jace Weaver in their co-authored work *American Literary Nationalism* by noting "Actually, Allen's work is quite the opposite [of their assertions]; instead of unfairly criticizing Western ideology as a monolith, Allen presents a nuanced analysis of the ways in which culture, gender and sexual orientation function as evidence of particular colonialist, patriarchal and homophobic ideologies."

Like Cox, Lisa Tatonetti also talks back to the insufficient recognition Paula's body of scholarship garners in contemporary discussions about Native American literary studies despite Paula being a primary crafter and leader of the discipline at its inception. Indeed, as Mann previously asserted, Paula was one of its founders. In an Interview format, Tatonetti candidly notes how easily scholars, particularly young scholars new to the academy, easily dismiss Allen's work because they have not been introduced to it. Following Tatonetti's interview is the final poem by Kristina Bitsue titled "Edge of Reality" that acknowledges the endurance of Indigenous traditions, people, and the cycles of Mother Earth. Bitsue reminds us through her Grandmother's practices that with offerings, human beings can be forgiven, and Earth can restore what has been broken.

The words of the literary scholar A. LaVonne Brown Ruoff close the collection with her review of Paula's posthumously published poetry collection *America the Beautiful: Last Poems* (West End Press 2010). In the Review, Ruoff describes Paula's final work as "a poignant tribute to the land and people she loved" and recounts Patricia Clark Smith's words from the collection. Ruoff notes that in "To the Reader," Smith writes "the manuscript was completed and sent to West End as Paula was awaiting the death she knew was coming from lung cancer." Ruoff has also graciously included the Eulogy she delivered at Paula's memorial service. With Ruoff's review and eulogy, the final threads of this anthology are drawn snugly together and joined with their beginnings. With Smith's and Paula's words a legacy greater than themselves is created from which readers generations from now can know "something good happened here among these people" and how the battle was waged as a community.

Bitsue's last photograph, "Anasazi Rooms," depicts a fundamental value of Pueblo culture to live and understand life within, and not separate from, the shape of the land. This ancient structure sits open to the sky of the southwest and invites readers into a living world that compels the imagination, just as Paula did. The view is bright upon the ancient land, just as those who see the future through the lens of Indigenous cultures know that nothing of beauty can ever be taken from us.

Portrait of Paula
10/24/1939–5/29/2008

Menoukha R. Case

Paula Gunn Allen

October 24, 1939–May 29, 2008

EDUCATION

Ph.D. 1975, American Studies, University of New Mexico/ Albuquerque

M.F.A. 1968, Creative Writing, University of Oregon/Eugene

B.A. 1966, English, University of Oregon/Eugene

AWARDS AND HONORS

Nomination for the Pulitzer Prize for the book, *Pocahontas*, 2004

Native Writers' Circle of the Americas Lifetime Achievement Award 2001.

Alumni Fellows Award for 2000-2001. Univ of Oregon CAS Alumni Advisory Council.

Hubbell Medal for Lifetime Achievement in American Literature, 1999.

American literature section of the Modern Language Association of America.

Honorary Doctor of Humanities, 1993. Mills College, Oakland, CA.

Wise Woman Award, 1992. Center for Policy on Women, Washington, D.C.

Vesta Award for Outstanding contributions in the Field of Scholarship, 1991. The Women's Building, Los Angeles, CA

Commendation from Lt Governor Leo McCarthy, State of California, 1991. Outstanding Contributions in the Literary Field.

Lesbian Rights Award, Southern CA Women for Understanding, 1991.

Native American Literature Prize for all works, 1990, sponsored by the Univ of CA/Santa Cruz.

American Book Award Before Columbus Foundation Nomination for *The Woman Who Owned the Shadows*, 1983.

Nomination for a Pushcart Poetry Prize, 1979 and 1981.

National Endowment for the Arts Creative Writing Award, 1977-78.

Julia Burgess Prize for Poetry, Univ of OR, 1967.

Kappa Kappa Gamma Prize for Poetry, Univ of NM, 1964.

TEACHING EXPERIENCE BEFORE RETIREMENT

Full Professor, Dept of English, American Indian Studies, Univ of CA/Los Angeles, 1990-1999

Full Professor, Native American Studies, Univ of CA/Berkeley, 1986-1990

RESEARCH AND WRITING FELLOWSHIPS

National Research Council Senior Post Doctoral Fellow for Minority Scholars, 1984-85. Assoc Fellow, Stanford Humanities Center.

Research Fellow, Institute of the Americas-American Indian Center of Research, UCLA, 1981-82.

National Endowment of the Arts Fellow, Creative Writing, 1977-78.

PUBLICATIONS

Pocahontas: Medicine Woman, Spy, Entrepreneur, Diplomat. New York: Harper, 2003.

Off the Reservation: Reflections of a Boundary-Busting, Border-Crossing, Loose Canon. Boston: Beacon Press, 1998.

As Long As the Rivers Flow: Biographies of Nine American Indians. With Patricia Clark Smith. NY: Scholastic Press, 1997.

Life is a Fatal Disease: Poems 1962-1995. LA: West End Press, 1997.

Song of the Turtle: American Indian Literature (1974-1994). NY: Ballantine Press, 1996.

Voice of the Turtle: American Indian Literature (1900-1970). NY: Ballantine Press, 1994.

Grandmothers of the Light: A Medicine Woman's Sourcebook. Boston: Beacon Press, 1991.

Spider Woman's Granddaughters: Short Stories by American Indian Writers. Boston: Beacon Press, 1989.

Skins and Bones. SF: West End Press, 1988.

Wyrds. SF: Taurean Horn Press, 1987.

The Sacred Hoop: Recovering the Feminine in American Indian Traditions. Boston: Beacon Press, 1986.

The Woman Who Owned the Shadows. Aunt Lute Books, 1983.

Studies on American Indian Literature: Critical Essays and Course Designs. NY: Modern Language Assoc, 1983.

A Cannon Between My Knees. NY: Strawberry Press, 1983.

Coyote's Daylight Trip. Albuquerque: La Confluencia, 1980.

Her final work, a poetry collection titled *America the Beautiful: Last Poems,* was published posthumously by West End Press in 2010.

Along with these monographs, Dr. Gunn Allen published over 75 scholarly articles, reviews, poetry and fiction in anthologies and journals such as *Recovering the World: Essays on Native American Literature,* the *Journal of the Modern Language Association, American Indian Culture and Research Journal, Sinister Wisdom, Multi-Ethnic Literature of the United States (MELUS), Calyx, Weaving the Visions:*

New Patterns in Feminist Spirituality, She Rises Like the Sun: Invocations of the Goddess by Contemporary American Women Poets, and *In A Different Light: An Anthology of Lesbian Writers,* among many others.

She was a sought-after speaker in both artistic and academic venues and lectured extensively across the United States and abroad. Some of these places include (in some cases multiple appearances over several years): Amherst College, New York State University, Writers In Performance Series of the Manhattan Theatre Club in New York City, Northwest Women's Studies Association, Women Writers of Color Series at Chico State University, Stanford University Poetry, Prose, and Politics Readers Series, Santa Cruz County National Organization for Women (spoke with Adrienne Rich, Grace Paley, Lucille Clifton, and Gloria Anzaldua), Modern Language Association national conference, Women's Institute for Theology and Nebraska Wesleyan University, Ithaca College, Dickinson College, Feminist Institute at the University of Illinois, and Association for Studies in American Indian Literature. She notes in her biographical materials that, strictly as a poet, she "participated in four marathon readings in several states, and have read over seventy other occasions as featured or invited poet."

WE REMEMBER

Old Beclabito
Kristina Bitsue

Paula Gunn Allen

A Retrospective

Barbara Alice Mann

Michael Dorris has often been identified as the originator of
Native American Studies as a university program, but I
credit Paula Gunn Allen for that task. Yes, Dorris did first institute something named "Native American Studies" at Dartmouth
in 1972, but it was really Paula who created the intellectual respect-
ability of the field with *The Sacred Hoop*, first published in 1986.
Before that time, NAS was waved off as a sop tossed not *to*, but *at*,
the Indian congeries hanging around the waning Civil Rights
Movement. After the *Hoop*, however, no one could successfully
pretend that there was no intellectual content to Native American
culture. Outrageous as that proposition seems today, it was
exactly the one that prevailed in yakademia at the time.

For her pains, Paula was subjected to nearly hysterical attacks
from the dead, white humanities establishment, and she was left
to weather the storm pretty much on her own. Those who had
succeeded in forcing a few Native perspectives into academia in
the 1970s—I am thinking particularly of Vine Deloria, Jr., here—
had the advantage of being male. Yes, Deloria, the Yankton
Nakota scholar who, along with Allen, drove Native America into
academic consciousness, suffered heavy attack, too, but his sex

was never instanced as part of his high crime in talking back to the Master Narrative. Moreover, since racists actually believe their own propaganda, I think the fact that Deloria came from a putatively "warrior" culture also helped moderate the yelping aimed at him. Euroamerican culture glorifies its racist ideal of the Indian warrior, resulting in a grudging respect for it, but Paula came from an agricultural, woman-friendly culture. To the racist-raider, "woman" means "weak," so she was seen as an easy target.

The purpose of such attacks is to inflict so much pain as to silence the pesky author rather conclusively. In various conversations that I had with Paula touching on the poundings that she took over *The Sacred Hoop*, I could see that the attacks had been very traumatic for her. In fact, before I published *Iroquoian Women*, she advised me to brace myself. "They are going to come after you with everything they have," she predicted. "Be sure you are ready for the death threats." Having received some of the same backlash as Paula, I can testify to her strength of character in having withstood it alone and even shaking it off. I can also thank her for valiantly having taken the brunt of the storm for those of us who followed. I have since gotten my share of threats, invective, and abuse, but I do believe it was not as horrifying as what Paula faced. People who walk out front always have the most and deepest wounds to show for their leadership.

I call her "Paula" not out of presumption but because she and I became intellectual buddies after we first met in 1999. She had been brought into the University of Toledo as a speaker by its women's center. Solely because of my Native American identity, which I thought a rather racist method of appointing committee members, I was pulled into the circle, after most of the event planning had been done. (I suspect that someone suddenly noticed that there were no Indians on the committee.) In consequence of being the committee's Token Indian, I was introduced to Paula at a small event the evening before her big speech. The next morning, I was to bring Paula to the auditorium for her advertised, public, mid-morning address, but when I arrived at her hotel at 7:30 A M., Paula was not ready to leave. Breakfast was on her mind.

"Have you eaten?" she asked, nodding toward the hotel's restaurant. I was a newly minted Ph.D., part-timing at the University for miserably low wages. "Can't afford that," I predicted. "I can," she said firmly, over my objections that the university would only reimburse her the per diem on *her* breakfast. "My treat, my treat." She dismissed all objections, dragging me down the hall to the dining area. "You're too skinny," she added, giving me the eyeball once-over.

I glanced at my watch. I was supposed to deliver Paula a good hour-and-a-half before she spoke. Apparently, it would take that long to show her where the podium was. "We don't have much time before they send the posse after us," I cautioned. "They'll wait," she assured me, glancing over the menu. Apparently, it did not meet with her expectations. "Now I *know* I'm in the Midwest!" Farmers' breakfasts are featured menu items around here.

Having hovered between poor and desperately poor my whole life, I have become pretty good at minimizing expenses. I ordered two eggs, over easy, with white toast. There might have been some link sausage involved. Coffee appeared.

"Nobody picked me up at the Detroit airport yesterday," Paula told her plate. "I kept waiting, thinking that there must have been some mistake, but no one ever came. About an hour from when I had to speak last night, I despaired and hired a cab. It cost me a lot. I figured the center would pick it up, but I was in such a rush,

I forgot to get a receipt when I jumped out of the cab and ran into the Student Union."

"*Nobody picked you up?*" I was pretty disturbed by that. Detroit is in a different *state* from Toledo. "Nope." She considered a forkful of food, but I was still chewing on the committee's having abandoned her in a strange airport. I should have known better than to allow a bunch of white feminists to plan the whole visit. They see Indians as toys, not real—unless one of us has the audacity to challenge one of their pet pretensions. Then, the only good Indian is a dead Indian.

As it turned out, Paula and I hit it off and sat talking for a long time after our plates had been decimated and cleared. The coffee flowed freely, to the growing ire of the waiter, who clearly wanted the table for Important Guests, not gabbing Indian women. Ignoring him, we canvassed everything from racism in academia to UFOs and suicide. Just before Paula had left for Toledo, her daughter (I believe it was) interrupted a suicide attempt and was now afraid that the rescued friend would never talk to her again.

"Death will do that, too," I observed casually. Paula let out a major yuk, smacked the table lightly, and quipped, "I just love talking to other Indians!" The waiter scowled. Paula ignored him. "Indians are so practical, cut right to the chase. If I had told the same story to a white woman, I would have had to sit here another hour canvassing everyone's feelings, the oppression that drives women to suicide, and whether anyone has a right to intervene."

On Indian time, we left for the auditorium around twenty minutes before Paula had to speak, which was just about enough time to drive her to the venue from the hotel. Indeed, we arrived just as the previous speaker was finishing and Paula was about to be introduced. The other committee members, evidently harried, spotted us entering the back of the hall and rushed bodily upon us. I thought we were under attack for a moment. They immediately dragged Paula away by both arms from my corrupting presence; one stayed behind to lecture me on the meaning of time. "We *are* on time," I objected, pointing to the stage. Paula's introduction had just concluded, and she stepped up to the mic. The women's center did not put me on another committee for about ten years.

During that same visit, Paula told me that she, too, had been forced to teach part-time, for lousy wages and no benefits for *several years* before UCLA formally hired her. This was *after* she had become quite famous for *The Sacred Hoop*, a book that had almost not appeared, at all. In the household of her youth, she said, being published by the Beacon Press was considered Sublime Authorial Success, so that, when she wrote the *Hoop*, she naturally directed it to Beacon. The original acquisitions editor did not think much of the manuscript and, in fact, had just stuffed it into a drawer, out-of-sight, out-of-mind. A new editor came in, cleaned out the desk, found the discarded manuscript, read it, and loved it. That is how *Hoop* hit the bookshelves. Paula wryly assured me that publishing was a crapshoot.

As it turned out, I already had a publisher for *Iroquoian Women: The Gantowisas*, but, because I was a nobody at the time, my editor wanted A Big Name to write the book's preface. Never shy about seizing an opportunity, I asked Paula whether she would consider writing my preface. To my surprise, without the slightest hesitation, she said, "Yes. When can you get me the manuscript?" It was quickly supplied.

Then, there was dead silence, first days of it, and next, weeks. The publisher was growing restless. I thought, *Paula is busy. She just hasn't gotten to it.* I emailed her. She emailed back. Nothing happened. My editor was pressing me, since *Iroquoian Women* was ready to go to print. When I finally reached Paula by phone to ask why she had not yet come forward with the preface, I expected anything but the answer she gave me.

"The book's too good," she said. "I'm overwhelmed by the scholarship in it. When you asked me for a preface, I had no idea what it was for. I assumed it would just be some little, nothing piece that no one would ever see. *That* book, though," she said with emphasis, "is going to be famous. I didn't think I could write anything good enough."

It hit me that Paula was having a crisis of self-confidence over my preface. After I got over my incredulity, we talked about my book for a while, with Paula pointing out this issue, that issue, and stray cogitations on some themes. "Why not write down what you just told me?" I suggested, and that is what Paula sat down, composed, and emailed to me that afternoon.

We remained in friendly communication thereafter, often discussing the American university as the last bastion of unabashed race privilege and elite, white entitlement. She would tell me one breath-taking story after another of the mistreatment that she had suffered during her tenure at UCLA, and I would respond with my own horror stories. Indians in academia are both isolated and besieged. We need all the mutual support we can get.

When Paula found herself besieged by her last enemy, cancer, we had been planning a joint book on genuine Native concepts of spirituality, as opposed to the heavily Christianized nonsense that passes for Indian spirituality among both academics and New Agers. She was planning to look at cultures west of the Mississippi, and I, at cultures east of it. We had agreed that nothing still held secret by the various medicine societies would be discussed. We were looking at overarching themes and conceptual frameworks. Paula wanted to shop the book to her publisher, HarperCollins, a trade publisher, before we went to my academic publisher, Praeger. She preferred HarperCollins' wider, more general distribution. Meantime, she wrote a chapter, "Does Euro-think Become Us?," for an anthology I was editing, *Daughters of Mother Earth* (out in paperback as *Make a Beautiful Way*).

Unfortunately, Paula then broke her wrist, which impeded any ability to type, and shortly afterward, she was hit by a terrible fire, which consumed all her books and papers. For a scholar to lose her life's work is no small blow, professionally and emotionally. Paula was just recovering from that setback when her cancer kicked into high gear. Sadly, she was never able to compose her half of the manuscript that we had planned together. If and when I do finish that book, I will certainly dedicate it to Paula.

For now, all I can do is page through my well-worn, much loved copy of *Hoop*, recalling the revelation it was when I first picked it up in 1986. At the time, I was not in academia, and had no plans to be, but was just trying to survive on the lousy jobs that this country allots to people of the wrong race, wrong sex, wrong class of origin, and wrong religion. Every page was a balm, confirming things that I already knew, but had never before seen in print. It dawned on me that I was not crazy, after all; America was. I should not, therefore, have been astonished when Paula told me that her first reaction upon reading the manuscript of *Iroquoian Women* was, "I'm not crazy, after all! I'm just Indian."

Dear Mentors

A Recollection

Janice Gould

I met Paula Gunn Allen around the time I was studying Linguistics at the University of California, Berkeley. Paula joined the
U.C. faculty in 1982, just before I earned my B.A. Though I did not
study with Paula, I read her poetry in *The Remembered Earth*,
edited by Geary Hobson. Some of her work spoke to me, and I
appreciated her humor, while other poems seemed to veer into
abstraction or to take up topics that I didn't connect with. Nevertheless, in the few years that I studied at Cal, Paula became something of a mentor to me, as did Hopi/Miwok poet Wendy Rose and
historian Clara Sue Kidwell, of Choctaw/Chippewa descent. As a
Native American student who was "older" and "non-traditional,"
getting to know other American Indian women in the academy was
encouraging and important to my sense of belonging.

My focus in Linguistics had been on American Indian languages,
and when I was accepted into the Ph.D. program, I knew it was an
exciting opportunity. But midway into my first semester as a doctoral student, I changed my mind about pursuing this career path.
I had resumed studying, writing, and publishing poetry, an old passion. I decided to apply to the Master's program in English at Berkeley with the idea of learning more about writing and literature.

Professor Janet Adelman, who directed the Masters students, accepted me into the program in 1984 and became my advisor. Janet wanted to introduce me to Patricia Clark Smith (Pat), a poet of Micmac descent whom she had known at Yale. Pat taught American Indian Literature at the University of New Mexico, and she was a good friend of Paula Gunn Allen. In fact, Pat had directed Paula's dissertation when Paula studied at UNM as a graduate student in American Studies. The core of that dissertation later became one of Paula's germinal works, *The Sacred Hoop: Recovering the Feminine in American Indian Traditions*, first published in 1986. It was a text that in many ways helped to shape my Master's thesis.

I had lived in my family home in the Berkeley Hills for many years when I started my studies at Cal. Gerald Vizenor began teaching Native American literature at U.C. Berkeley around the time I became a graduate student there. He lived not far from me in Clara Sue Kidwell's house. Vizenor and I would sometimes walk to campus together, down the steep, winding streets. A few times I sat in on his literature class, which had a different feel from the literature classes I was taking in English. Every class I took or audited while at Berkeley offered new insights and understandings. I found the validity of writers of color—especially Native American writers— to be valuable since many shared my own mixed-blood experience.

Also around 1984, I met Beth Brant, who would edit *Gathering of Spirit: A Collection by North American Indian Women* (eventually published in 1989). I believe Beth was in California to attend a writing conference, "Women's Voices," which took place in Santa Cruz. That volume was an important "first," as it included writing by lesbian Native American poets such as Paula, Chrystos, Beth, me, and others. At that time, Paula was romantically involved with poet Judy Grahn and living in San Pablo, a bay area suburb north of Berkeley. I didn't really know this until Judy gave a memorable reading in Dwinelle Hall on the Berkeley campus, with Paula in the audience. Then it dawned on me that they were a couple, and I remember being surprised. Knowing that Paula was a "sister" probably gave me the courage to ask her if she would read and critique some of my poems, which she consented to do. We met at the Mediterranean Café for coffee a few weeks later. "Your poems are all Zen, Zen, Zen," she told me. "And then suddenly they connect, and there's the earth, the sky, your family, your lovers." I had no idea what she was talking about, and wasn't sure if being "Zen" was a good thing or not, but I was too shy to ask.

The Bay Area was home to and attracted many other women writers of color during this period: Cherríe Moraga, Gloria Anzaldúa, Ana Castillo, Nellie Wong, Merle Woo, Angela Davis, and June Jordan, to name a few. Many of these writers my soon-to-be-partner Marie-Elise (Mimi) Wheatwind and I invited to speak in a graduate English class we put together at U.C. Berkeley titled "Literature by North American Women of Color." While this course was initially an elective, it later became a core class in English, and to get it off the ground (it was 1986), we needed a faculty sponsor. Sue Schweik, a young professor with whom I had studied the year before, stepped forward to fulfill this role. Paula was one of many women professors teaching at Berkeley who generously donated an evening to speak with us during that semester. Paula had a certain dignity, and though friendly, always spoke with authority. I recall that she talked about the research and writing she had done for *The Sacred Hoop*.

That same year, at the urging of Janet and Pat, I applied to the doctoral program in American Studies at the University of New Mexico. I had met Pat in January, when I traveled to Albuquerque to visit my older sister, who lived in northern New Mexico. Pat met me at the old Albuquerque airport (now the "Sunport") and took me to lunch at Monroe's, an established New Mexican eatery on Lomas Boulevard, near Old Town. She regaled me with stories about Paula, Leslie Silko, Joy Harjo, Luci Tapahonso, Geary Hobson, Louis Owens, and other notables in the world of Native American literature who were or had been in Albuquerque.

After Mimi and I moved to that city, in May 1987, Pat welcomed us in her exuberant and kindly way. She drove us around Albuquerque and showed us where Paula had once lived in a seemingly out-of-place log cabin. It sat on a treeless plot of land near old adobe houses in the North Valley, off of Rio Grande Boulevard. Another time, Pat took us out to the back roads around Laguna Pueblo to show us the place where Night Swan's tavern had once stood. Night Swan, a colorful and compassionate character in Leslie Silko's novel *Ceremony*, was an old flamenco dancer, and the main character, Tayo's, first lover. I remember thinking, "So this is where Paula and Leslie grew up, out here under this hot sun—in one of these little villages!" It seemed so humbling to me as an aspiring writer that these vitally important women came from what seemed such a remote and rural place at the foot of Mt. Taylor. On another excursion, Pat carted us up to Jemez Pueblo and eagerly pointed out a run-down gas station in San Ysidro with its oval red and white Conoco sign. This was where Abel, the main character in N. Scott Momaday's novel, *House Made of Dawn*, had stepped off the bus to meet his grandfather, who had come in a wagon to drive him home.

Pat's ancestry, like my own, was Irish and French. Perhaps it was her drop of Micmac blood, as much as associating with Paula, that helped her realize how the earth was storied, not just with legends from the oral tradition of the Southwest Indian tribes, but with current tales and histories some of them written, and some of them spoken with laughter, or with deep sorrow and dismay.

Paula returned often to New Mexico to visit family, and whenever she showed up, Pat called to let me know that Paula was in town. I remember once having coffee with Paula at the Frontier Restaurant during one of her trips home. As we were conversing, she asked if I ever wrote fiction. "Not often," I told her. "Give me something," she said, encouraging me to try. She added that she was leaving at the end of the week so I should get some writing to her soon. I brought a story to her a few days later and she wanted to publish it as is. Because of its personal content, I felt hesitant and vulnerable, but Paula, being a lesbian, understood, and suggested I come up with a pseudonym. So "Stories Have No Endings" by Misha Gallagher was published in her volume, *Spider Woman's Granddaughters*.

Another time when Paula was visiting, she invited Mimi and me to breakfast. She was about to leave town, and wanted us to meet her mom. We joined them at Garcia's on Central Avenue for *huevos rancheros* with blue corn tortillas and green *chile*. I remember that Mimi brought some old chapbooks—some of Paula's earliest publications, *The Blind Lion* and *Star Child*, and asked Paula to sign them. Paula was surprised and delighted, and her mom passed her hand over the covers and paged through these books thoughtfully as we talked. It was a sweet and comfortable occasion, and I think almost every time I saw Paula after that, she would look at me and, with a little smile, tell me that I reminded her of her Isleta relatives. Not too long after that Paula's mom passed away, and even though we had met her but once, Mimi and I felt sad we would not see her again.

Mimi and I had been living in Albuquerque for some years when Paula moved back to the state. She was briefly part of our writer's group that Margaret Randall had initiated with a few women writers who lived in the region at the time, including Joy Harjo and Luci Tapahonso. Pat, a wonderful writer, was part of this group too. A short list of her literary accomplishments includes a book of poems, *Changing Your Story*, as well as the young adult book, *Weetamoo: Heart of the Pocassets*, and another that she co-wrote with Paula, *As Long as the Rivers Flow: The Stories of Nine Native Americans*. Pat also beautifully translated a series of sonnets by Plutarch, though I'm not certain any were published.

Albuquerque's literary community was lively, and people with strong personalities dropped in and out of it. Because Pat's husband, John Crawford, owned and operated West End Press, there were book launch parties from time to time, where such writers as Jim Sagel, Ana Castillo, Lorna Dee Cervantes, nila northSun, and others would show up. We had parties at our home in the North Valley, too, where I would play my accordion or guitar. People would sing together, songs like "De Colores" and "Union Maid," or country favorites like "There's a Tear in My Beer" or "Your Cheatin' Heart." Both Pat and Paula loved to sing. I remember that Paula particularly enjoyed "La Llorona." She would sit pensively listening when I played it on my accordion, sometimes singing in a husky voice any words she could recall.

Later, when Paula started teaching at UCLA, it seems to me she "commuted" back and forth from L.A. to Albuquerque. I remember her telling us that Ken Lincoln had been commuting in this way, living in Santa Fe, but teaching at UCLA a couple of times a week, so she knew it could be done. After Paula's father died, she moved back to California. It was a time in Paula's life that Pat referred to as her "Hollywood Phase." Paula lost a lot of weight during this period, was looking something like a glamour girl. She had rented a white Mercedes convertible to drive around in. We met her in Anaheim once during her "Hollywood Phase." The American Booksellers Association (ABA) convention took place there at the end of May, 1992. Mimi was working for Salt of the Earth Books then, an important political and multicultural bookstore in Albuquerque owned by John Randall. That bookstore brought in some renowned authors, and some who were rising stars: Julia Alvarez, Michael Dorris, Demetria Martinez, Elena Poniatowska, Isabel Allende, Jimmie Santiago Baca, Terry Tempest Williams, and Sherman Alexie, to a name a few. John helped the bookstore workers get to Anaheim, and I came along that trip because I was invited by John, one of the co-founders of Booksellers for Social Responsibility, to give a reading. The panel I was on included Judith Freeman, Eduardo Galeano, and Barbara Kingsolver.

John Crawford's West End Press had a booth on the Convention Center floor, and somehow it was arranged that Paula would drive over from L.A. and meet John Crawford, Mimi, and me for breakfast at a place on West Katella Avenue. We met at John's hotel and Paula drove us in her Mercedes—with the top down! There we were on a balmy, beautiful, not-too-smoggy morning, cruising with Paula, who was chain smoking at the wheel, a pert brimmed hat on her head.

If Paula had tried to quit smoking, I know she wasn't successful. I remember her once laughing off her addiction to cigarettes. "Tobacco," she announced, "is a sacred plant." But it occurred to me later that when the sacred is abused—addiction is an abuse of the body, and of the plant, too—it may turn against us.

In the late 1990s Mimi and I left New Mexico for jobs in another state, and I was in touch with Paula only occasionally by email or phone. I remember once visiting her in Berkeley after she had retired from UCLA. She was living in a southwest corner of town in an old run-down apartment that looked like it belonged in Tucson or Albuquerque. I could see her health was not good; she suffered from emphysema, and she had gained a lot of weight.

A couple of years later, during a visit to see my sister in New Mexico, I stopped overnight to see Pat and John. Paula had recently traveled from California to be with them for a few nights. I remember an oxygen tank still sitting on the front stoop of their North Valley home. Pat had tried to clear the smoke smell out of the room where Paula had slept, and where I would now sleep, and even though it had been well over a week, everything was saturated with the smell of cigarettes. Pat and I both felt terrifically sad that our friend was caught in such an onerous addiction, a trap that she could not escape.

Pat grieved Paula's death in May 2008, but we both sadly agreed that it was expected. A year later, I drove down to Albuquerque from Colorado, where I now live, to visit Pat. She had asked me to drive her and another friend, who was visiting from the east, out to Acoma. Up on the mesa top, under a wide, blue sky, Pat and I reminisced about Paula. I noticed my friend was out of breath and unsteady on her feet. Though she wasn't feeling well, Pat wanted her east coast acquaintance to experience the New Mexican landscape. As we drove back toward Interstate 40, she suggested that we drive out to Cubero to see where the Francis family used to live (Paula's maiden name was Paula Francis, and her father had been the Lieutenant Governor of New Mexico). It was so like Pat to want to tell us stories about Paula and her family, to show us this country that held so many memories. We drove back to Albuquerque along old Highway 66, and stopped briefly in Laguna to see where the Marmon's store had been. Pat's east coast friend had not seen this country before, had not heard tales about Pat and Paula's friendship, built out of love for stories, the land, children, families.

Ironically, the dear friend who brought Pat and me together, Janet Adelman, also died of lung cancer. This was in April 2010. Janet was not a smoker. (Coincidentally, she passed on the same day as former Cherokee Chief Wilma Mankiller). Janet was a wonderful Shakespearian scholar, and I remember Pat saying she was one of the most insightful and compassionate people she knew. Pat's friendship with her was built around a mutual love for learning and literature, family and children (they both had two sons). Pat often told this story about their friendship: When Janet was pregnant with her first son, her husband, Bob, conspired to fly Pat out to Berkeley as a surprise so she could be with her best friend and help her through those first days of motherhood.

Unlike Paula's death, Janet's occurred rapidly, within three short months. I know that Pat was devastated by this, especially coming relatively soon after Paula's death. The following month, Pat called me to say that she had ordered rose bushes and had planted them in her yard in memory of Paula and Janet, a characteristically sweet and thoughtful gesture. Yet Pat herself was facing a difficult health situation, and in July—only weeks after she had called to tell me about the roses—Pat, too, crossed over to the spirit world.

It has been heartbreaking to lose these three brilliant colleagues, who were also my friends. I had thought they would be a part of my life as wise elders for many more years. I cherish memories of these lovely women who, I know, had their struggles and triumphs. For me, and for many, they were kind mentors and firm supporters, and beyond that, dear human beings.

On *Lubnaan* With Paula Gunn Allen

LeAnne Howe

I first met Paula Gunn Allen in the spring of 1985. She was reading with two other Native writers, Leslie Silko and local author Roxy Gordon (Choctaw descent) at the former cattle baron's mansion, Thistle Hill in Fort Worth, Texas. It was an exciting event because in 1985 Native writers in Texas were as rare as hen's teeth. The reading sponsored by the University of Texas at Arlington and organized by professor Kenneth Roemer was one of many Native events he'd planned that spring. Ken Roemer was and continues to be a strong ally of Native writers.

Paula Gunn Allen's presentation at Thistle Hill was titled, "Whose Dream Is This Anyway?" Leslie Silko read from her seminal work *Ceremony* and Roxy Gordon followed her by reading from *Breeds*, a memoir in stories. Yet, the thrill for all of us was that two generous, nationally recognized Native intellectuals had come to Dallas/Fort Worth to read to us from their work. Both Silko and Allen would go on to publish their defining works, *Almanac of the Dead* (Silko, 1991) and *The Sacred Hoop* (Allen, 1986). But the year is 1985 and their works and the books of dozens by Native women writers are yet to come.

That night in 1985 at Thistle Hill the audience was painfully thin.

Although we were in "Cowtown," the nickname for Fort Worth, Texas, a place that bills itself as "where the West begins," it does not include Indians so reading audiences weren't used to coming out to hear American Indians.

I also read that night from my newest short story, but I could not remember why I had the hubris to read before two women I admired. I wrote Ken Roemer and asked what possessed me to read. He emailed back. "Roxy knew your writing, and—I think he suggested that you read. We all enthusiastically agreed. So you performed before Leslie and Paula. Tiny audience but good times."

After the reading at Thistle Hill, Paula sat down with Roxy and me to talk about the future of Native literature(s), her own work, and her large family of educators and writers, brother Lee Francis and sister Carol Lee Sanchez. She also mentioned that she was part Lebanese, and that she had a *Jidoo*, grandfather in Arabia. I said that I had always wanted to go to Lebanon and that people often mistook me for Lebanese rather that Choctaw. It was then Paula asked if I would give her the short story I'd read from, "An American In New York." She said she was putting together a short story collection by Native women. I was flattered and honored that she wanted it. I gave her the copy I'd read from. Roxy told her about our new plays that we were working on together, *Big PowWow*, and *Indian Radio Days*. She told him to send her our new plays and what else we were working on. I believe he did that. Probably those copies of our work are in Paula's archive, and most likely Roxy's archive. (He died in 2000.)

Later that night we all parted ways. I went back to writing short stories and in 1987 Roxy and I had our first play *Big PowWow* produced by Sojourner Truth Theater in, of all places, the White

Elephant Saloon in Cowtown. (Yes, for the most part we had good audiences and the review in the Fort Worth Star Telegram was amazing.) The play ran for six weeks beginning in April through June 15, 1987, and was the first theatrical collaboration between American Indians and African-Americans in Texas. I never heard from Paula again. Then early one Sunday morning a friend of mine, Roy Hamric, professor at University of Texas at Arlington called. "Go to the newsstand right now and get a copy of *The New York Times Book Review.*"

"What for?" I asked.

"*Spider Woman's Granddaughters* is out, a collection of short stories edited by Paula Gunn Allen and you're in it!"

Like a shot, (and I'm not kidding) I drove to a local newsstand and bought the Sunday *NYT* and whipped through the pages of the Book Review. In the May 14, 1989 was a full-page story, "Above All Keep the Tale Going," by Ursula K. Le Guin. She wrote a detailed and glowing review of *Spider Woman's Granddaughters* and talked about the way Paula had sectioned the book with sub-headings, Part One: The Warriors, Part Two: The Causalities, Part Three: The Resistance. Le Guin had ended her book review with my work in the last paragraphs:

> Indian Humor is probably the quietest and driest in the world. The title of LeAnne Howe's 1987 story "An American in New York" is a good example. Her narrator goes on a "high-stakes bone business" to the Big Apple; it doesn't take long for the worm to turn. "No wonder we sold the whole place for twenty-six dollars and some beads," she remarks. She talks to immigrants—an Irishman after the good life, a Nigerian cab driver who wants to "do something" about the

plight of Native Americans. When she gets to the Statue of Liberty, she decides that Emma Lazarus was really an Indian.

"Give me your tired, your poor, your huddled masses yearning to breathe free."

"You did," says the narrator. "Now where do we go from here?" (15, *NYT Book Review*, 1989)

I was flabbergasted—and proud—that I was included in the book that featured Linda Hogan, Anna Lee Walters, Elizabeth Cook-Lynn, Leslie Silko, Soge Track, Louise Erdrich, Vickie L. Sears, Janice Gould as well as our elder writing sisters, Zitka-la-Sa, E. Pauline Johnson, and Ella Cara Deloria. I was all the more surprised because I didn't know anything about the book, or that my story had been accepted for publication. Nothing.

The next day I called Paula at her home in California and she answered. After congratulating her on the book (I'd bought one from a local bookstore) I said. "I'm also calling because I didn't know about the book, nor have I signed a contract allowing Beacon Press to publish my short story."

"Oh. Didn't we get a signed release from you?"

"No, I never heard from you. Also Choctaw is misspelled throughout the book."

Silence.

"I must have used an old English spelling of the tribe," she said.

"But we're one of the largest tribes in America. Can the press fix that in their next printing?"

To say I was naïve about the publishing business is an understatement. Paula laughed and said probably not. I was sad; thinking how other Choctaws might read the story and think it was my mistake. (I repeat. I was naïve.)

Paula brushed aside my concerns of publishing a story without my permission. "No one wanted your story, but I fought for you to be in the collection. I wanted it because it is different."

"Oh." That really hurt, but I was glad to hear she had fought for my story. She said she would send me a contract to sign and I agreed to backdate it.

That was that, and I don't think we ever talked about it again. Paula said there was going to be a reading at the Manhattan Theatre Club in New York City in March 1990 for the Writers in Performance Series. Would I come?

"Yes. I'll be there."

"There is no money to pay you to get there, or to stay overnight, but it would be good for your career, and I'll be introducing you to the audience. Joy Harjo, Janice Gould, Vickie Sears, and Beth Brant will be reading. You should come."

In March my boyfriend and I drove 1000 miles to New York City from Iowa City, IA. But I failed to get the exact address from Paula of where the Manhattan Theatre Club was located. We had a street map of NYC, and I'd booked a B&B for one night somewhere close to where I believed the theater was. Two friends, Kendall McCook, a local Texas author and poet Charlie Moon, a woman I'd met through Roxy Gordon, were going to be in New York City and written they would come to the reading. We were to meet up before the reading at the address I'd found by calling the Manhattan Theatre Club's office. Unfortunately it was their booking office. By the time we realized our mistake I only had one hour to find the venue in a city I was totally unfamiliar with. Fortunately Charlie remembered where the club "might" be. She'd lived in New York City a couple of years during the late 1980s. We made our way there by stopping to ask New Yorkers where Manhattan Theatre Club was located. At 7:55 PM. I walked into club with my friends in tow and Paula Gunn Allen was the first person I recognized.

"Where have you been? Never mind. You're going on first."

She introduced me and I read with all the passion of a person who'd been lost and afraid I'd never make it to the reading. I read with all the passion I could, remembering Paula's words, "No one wanted your story." I read with all the passion I could muster hoping the audience could hear my story was about New York, a place that had forgotten its Native beginnings. I wanted to make Paula proud that she'd fought for my story.

What I do remember about that night is the audience liked the story. I remember Native performers, Hortensia and Elvira, the Colorado Sisters of Coatlique Theater stood up and applauded. Soon the rest of the audience was standing. For me it was a night I would never forget. Joy, Janice, Beth Brant and Vickie Sears read from their work and it remains one of the highlights of my life. Beth Brant and Vickie Sears have both passed on and taken the holy road, as has Paula. I miss them all, and the camaraderie

I felt that night. Camaraderie is not the right word. I felt that we were sisters, a family of women writers coming together to share ourselves.

By this time you are probably wondering what links Paula Gunn Allen and *Lubnaan*, (Lebanon), with *Spider Woman's Granddaughters*. After the reading that night Paula again sat and talked with us. She and Jim Wilson began speaking about Lebanon and her Lebanese grandfather. Jim had lived in Beirut, Lebanon for nearly ten years. He began speaking Arabic greetings to Paula Gunn Allen, and she would answer him in Arabic. She spoke of her grandfather and the things *Jidoo* had taught her about Lebanon. Her eyes twinkled as she remembered him and it was in this small moment at the back of the Manhattan Theatre Club that I saw the young girl she must have been. How as Native women we have been integrating immigrants into our families for generations. This is the true strength of *Spider Woman's Granddaughters*.

Some twenty-one years later I would finally make it to Lebanon when I had a Fulbright Scholarship to Jordan in 2011. As I walked along the Corniche in Beirut, overlooking the Mediterranean, I thought of Paula Gunn Allen and that night when the stars aligned and I was lucky enough to meet her. To paraphrase LeGuin, "Above all, she kept the tale going."

Paula Gunn Allen & Mary TallMountain

Trickster, Jester, Clown . . .

Gabrielle Welford & Elaine Jacobs

Laughing women
                    the two of you
held by mountains
                    rivers   sky
arms about
                    each others' shoulders
dancing
                    the slow dance
                            of women,
                            friends.

Keep the water level,
                    The earth,
        with your feet
                    moving.
Hold the
horizon
                    steady as you
                            make the circle
                    with
                            your arms.

I have been
    surely blessed
        surely kept
        awake
  safe
in your circle.

—\/—

As anyone who knew her will tell you, Paula Gunn Allen (like her friend Mary TallMountain) was a kickass clown. In the style of one of her "important people," G.I. Gurdjieff, she believed in having fun playing with the energy of the universe and often, without warning, she slipped into her jester outfit to tweak the minds and spirits around her—including ours, her friends and students.

Where are you, Paula? And Mary! Like the twins—dancing in the sky, under earth, at two places in the same moment, moving backwards and forwards in time, switching off between beaming matriarch and devilish trickster. Both of you ill for so long in devastating ways—as you said of Mary, Paula: " . . . " Each of you must have switched bodies several times.

I met Paula in 1979 in Albuquerque, at the Siren Coffeehouse poetry readings she helped organize. She sat outside at a small table sometimes giving psychic readings. She gave me a reading that reverberates to this day—and was true for both of us: "Learn to nurture yourself." She had to become more guileful later on, as her fame spread and she joined prestigious institutions, to obscure her dual (only dual?) identity as respected academic and psychic madonna, as she had also to negotiate the landscapes of Native American scholar and teacher, Indian/Lebanese/Scottish woman (she called herself a "multicultural event") and lesbian.

Mary was living 20 minutes south of me in Petaluma when I was completing my M.A. in English at Sonoma State University in California. I spent a summer of days with her, talking, laughing, reading each other's poetry. I wrote five papers about her work, two of which have been published.

With these women, despite the pain, there was always laughter. Even in anger, laughter. It was the punctuation of all conversation. Aphasia, laughter. Sciatica, laughter. Alcoholism, near suicide, laughter. Cancer, laughter. Death and laughter, dancing. And sudden psychic movement into animal bodies—Mary's wolverine and wolf. Paula looking sideways and licking her chops. Watch out!

Toward the end of her days, Paula and I exchanged readings. I saw her leaning out the door of a flying locomotive engine, waving and grinning. "Your job is to have fun—through it all," I told her. She surely did her best. Confined to bed, for a long time unable even to raise her head without deathly dizziness, she kept grinning and quipping. Whenever Mary, the consummate writer, came up with one word for another because of her aphasia—"elephant," she said—"uncle," she meant—she roared with laughter.

And the clowning wasn't just the other side of pain. Perhaps one of the reasons Gurdjieff was Paula's chosen "master" for teaching middle class white women tribal values was his humor, his trickster nature. She told us about his painting sparrows yellow and selling them as canaries as he and his followers traveled about Russia, and other stories of imaginative tricksterism. Later, she told me she had to re-think his teachings after she had realized the ponderous seriousness of Gurdjieff's scribe, Ouspensky. Ouspensky has to be shaken out and humorized, read out of the corner of the eye, to make Gurdjieffian sense.

Paula possessed an uncanny ability to always leap beyond the accepted, out beyond the norm. Ask her any question, one with a fairly predictable answer, and you'd find yourself flying (in that locomotive engine?) blithely through a sky filled with energy portals, Tesla coils, pole reversals, acceptance of the impossible. A friend interviewed her about being gay and brought up the term, "two spirit," a proffered new word for LGBT Natives, and Paula scoffed at the idea of inventing some new word to try and float away from an uncomfortable reality.

She was always *for* reality, however wretched. She was the one who taught me to accept and start from the place where I am. Americans always want to be somewhere else, she said to us. To move, you can only start from where you are. As she became more ill, she always worked, kept working, at staying with the often grim reality. And, like Mary, she laughed and joked, dyed her hair red, had her nails beautifully done and painted by her loyal and likewise tricksterish home help, just days before she died.

What is the role of the jester, even of the more mundane clown? In my mind, it is a kind of jerking of the rug of reality, the kind of thing that happens when the cat crosses the doorway twice in the movie "The Matrix." Paula called these moments "fnords," and good jesters—Paula, Mary, G.I. Gurdjieff—will perceive and use the precise moment to open a window into a different and reality-changing view of the familiar. Shock and laughter! Magic!

Shifting a set-in-her-ways human being from one way of experiencing reality into another one, or giving her the information to shift herself, using what Gurdjieff called a "shock," is work for a trickster. When she was teaching at the Ethnic Studies Department at U.C. Berkeley, Paula set out to do this for a group of women when we began meeting in 1984. The group started as a formal series of classes at Mama Bear's, a women's coffeeshop in Oakland, California. When the class was over, we moved to Paula's house in El Sobrante, meeting for the next three years, finally several times a week.

... and Way Over a Rainbow: A Memoir of P.G.A.'s Non-Academic Teaching

It was one of those airless summer evenings in Oakland, California in 1984, when the fog veils everywhere with an eerie still. I figured to relieve my boredom with a jaunt over to Mama Bear's Wimmins' Bookstore, The East Bay hangout for the hip and queer and happening for at least a generation. Little could I have known that I was about to embark on the wildest quest of my already odd life, and never be bored again. Perusing the bulletin board under the front desk, I was immediately drawn to a bright orange flyer advertising the start of an Urban Dyke Rainbow Warriors Class. Huh? I could relate to urban and dyke, felt a bit misfit by rainbow, being white, but warrior? I was a veteran of many an anti-war demonstration by then and felt more than skeptical, but something about that outrageous title was beguiling. There was a brief blurb outlining a wide-ranging Spiritual study program and it was offered by a U.C.-Berkeley Professor whom I'd never heard of, a Dr. Paula Gunn Allen. I asked Carol behind the desk about it and she assured me that Paula was well worth listening to. Truer words were never heard.

Dr. Gunn Allen opened the first class with a brief bio—author, poet, teacher, mother, lesbian, grew up on the Laguna Pueblo Indian Rez with her mother's people, and her Lebanese Catholic father. Clearly aware of how off-putting that "warrior" word was, (probably intentionally so) she clarified its usage within an Indian mind-set as something like impeccable integrity and a fierce purpose. She next explained that she intended to lead us through a detailed survey of some of the more obscure Spiritual traditions—at least so to the mostly "middle-class white girls" arrayed before her, notebooks and pens poised—and that she expected us to purchase and read a lot of dense books. That thinned the herd quickly (also intended), but for those of us who persevered, an education both scholarly and ephemeral changed our beings deeply, forever. Weekly, for the next several years, Paula expounded on quite a number of Native American Indian stories, spirituality, and social structures, Theosophical principles, the nature and practice of magick, E.S.P., and lucid dreaming, and the intensive inner Fourth Way Work of Georg Ivanovitch Gurdjieff.

One of my favorite memories is of the moonless night her Rainbow Warrior students (about 40 by then) stepped solemnly in procession around her back yard in El Cerrito, dedicating the Earth there for a planned Mystery School. Paula had taught us about the power of Indigenous masks that if created in a mindful and sacred manner the wearer could truly be transformed. During the previous week's class, as we drew and decorated our paper grocery bag masks, I reminded myself that Paula had quoted Mr. Gurdjieff that if one is not a skeptic by nature there's no use in pursuing Spiritual Work. I suppose to a casual on-looker that slow parade of bag-headed people might have caused chortles, but I knew, with a growing certainty as foot was placed after intentional foot, that the one wearing my mask was definitely not the same "I" that my job coworkers thought they knew. I felt huge, dispassionate, like some Easter Island stone statue. Even more amazing, when I looked through the eye-holes at the other students I could see that they were also changed—actually appearing much larger than in "real" life and indiscernible as to who was inside which mask despite my having watched them draw and don them. Doctor Gunn (as I'd come to affectionately call her, knowing her own affection for her Scottish "Uncle Gunn") was standing to the side of our circle holding some of her favorite flowers and twigs from her yard, radiating a visible pinkish glow, her eyes gleaming bright as the moonlight on the far side.

Another of her notable experiments was teaching us in dreams. She told our class that while settling into bed on a certain night we should make an intention of attending her class during sleep. Holding my inadequacy fears at bay that night, I did as instructed and fell asleep. Quite to my surprise my dream-self walked up to a building and entered to find a classroom of fellow students, some of whom I recognized. Paula was standing at the front of the class and lecturing. I honestly couldn't recall the topic when I awoke the next morning, but vaguely thought I'd learned a lot. At our next regular class meeting a couple days later she asked if we'd gotten to the dream class. About half of us acknowledged that we were there, some remembering various bits of her lecture. She seemed pleased with the results and convened a few more dream classes over the years, with more of us recalling more of the specifics each time. Dr. Gunn Allen is certainly a far more accomplished teacher than even her many well-deserved academic accolades tell us.

At some point a number of students asked for a "church" to be established so others could participate who couldn't attend the weekly classes. With the generous and enthusiastic consent of Carol and Alice at Mama Bear's, Paula obligingly established Sunday morning services there, based in ritual, complete with a sermon (a "haggle") she prepared or invited a guest speaker (often one of us) to present. Every Sunday we bestowed red roses to menstruating womyn and white roses to the elders in ceremonies with poems honoring them. We recited prayers she wrote and sang all sorts of songs, sometimes with a guitar or violin a student brought. These events always concluded with a well-arrayed feast and spirited conversations as we lingered long after the hour allotted. Out of this community "ministry" developed special services for bereavement and coupledom, and certain students volunteered to officiate, creating appropriate ritual for each occasion.

Paula's phenomenal reputation quickly grew along the Bay Area womyn's grapevine and within a couple of years she had more eager Warriors than she wanted to teach in a single class. She established four subsets she called Clans, aligned with the directions, and asked four of her most experienced students to lead one of each. (I was typecast appropriately in the West, Heyokah, the rebel clown.) We Clan Mothers did our best to instruct the many new students who arrived every few months in the basics of the mountain of information that Dr. Gunn Allen had so benevolently blessed us with through countless hours of formal classes, dinner parties, and one-on-one intensive sessions tailored to each of our talents and interests. I marvel at her ability and willingness to share so much, especially as it was in addition to what must have been a full and grinding schedule at the University for her many "regular" classes. What words are there for such a deep well of gratitude to a teacher who gathered girls and inspired goddesses?

I had a dream this morning.

I was Working—always Working—in a laboratory. I needed another, fancier, tool for diagnosis. I went to the Boss with my request. In Paula's office I asked, please, for the Higher Tool. She agreed, matter of fact, no "considering" needed. We searched together for Diag(onal)Gnosis tools. Sideways across the Cross— she never went straight—a very Fancy Dancer.

Dr. Gunn teaches Being. Not thinking, feeling, or even doing. Those are human attributes to be watched, not claimed. No analysis, judgment, or changing of behavior. Stand, flat-footed, bottom tucked under spine, chin tucked over it, OBSERVE. See what IS, now. Revelation explodes in a simple I AM. She is. We are. ALL IS, was, will BE.

I suspect that few are aware that along with her well-deserved accolades for her writings and academic teaching, Dr. Paula Gunn Allen is a superior Teacher of G.I. Gurdjieff's "Fourth Way" spiritual path. She quotes "the old man" often, and the Prophet (Peace be upon him), with the cheek-tongued reverence they'd probably appreciate. She feeds our Rainbow Warriors class on *Beelzebub's Tales*, Ouspensky and Blavatsky, Pueblo and Navajo stories, and Rumi's poems for dessert. She teaches in myth and ritual, science experiments and art projects, and in Dreams, Visions, voices from Mesa and Mountains.

I will not write of my teacher in the past tense. Shimanna lives. Storm clouds always gather moisture somewhere, fill parched arroyos with turbulent life. Diaphanous clouds of fog always caress some shifting coastline, straddling solidity and liquidity, forever.

Do not seek for metaphors. I only tell true tales.

Paula Gunn Allen

Innovator of New Academic Disciplines

Annette Van Dyke

Paula Gunn Allen is considered to be one of the founders of women's/Native American spirituality as an academic discipline. Spirituality is central to her work, underpinning her championing of the restoration of gay and lesbian Native Americans to their rightful place. She was an early advocate of the idea that being gay or lesbian in a Native American culture was a spiritual calling, while being perfectly aware of contemporary challenges to that position. By exploring the evolution of her career as scholar, writer, and professor, we can follow the changes in the intertwining fields of Native American/ women's spirituality and lesbian studies.

Her early scholarly work, her dissertation: "Sipapu: A Cultural Perspective" (1975) became the exceedingly influential *The Sacred Hoop: Recovering the Feminine in American Indian Traditions* (1986). This text contains her 1975 germinal essay, "The Sacred Hoop: A Contemporary Perspective," which was one of the first to detail the ritual function of Native American literatures as opposed to Euro-American literatures. *The Sacred Hoop* is considered a foundation for not only the study of Native American gender, but also for the study of culture and Native literature. Drawing upon Allen's own experience as a Laguna Pueblo woman, it calls attention to her belief in the power of the oral tradition now embodied in contemporary Native American literature to effect healing, survival, and continuance.[3] Further, Allen's work discusses not only the importance of women in her own society, but also across the Native American panorama and through time.

Allen wrote from the perspective of a Laguna Pueblo woman from a culture in which the women are held in high respect. The descent is matrilineal—women owned the houses, and the primary deities are female. A major theme of Allen's work is delineation and restoration of this woman-centered culture. Elaborating on the roles and power of Native American women, Allen's "Who is Your Mother: Red Roots of White Feminism" came out in *Sinister Wisdom* in 1984. In this startling article, Allen articulated Native American contributions to democracy and feminism, countering a popular idea that a society in which women's power was equal to men's never existed.

She also has been a major champion to restore the place of gay and lesbian Native Americans, explaining their power as spiritual to be used for the good of the community. These ideas were first published in a groundbreaking essay in *Conditions*, "Beloved Women: Lesbians in American Indian Cultures," (1981) and then reworked for the *Sacred Hoop*.

Her work abounds with the mythic dimensions of women's relationship to the sacred, as well as the struggles of contemporary Native American women, many of whom have lost the respect formerly accorded to them because of the incursion of EuroAmerican

---

3 Some of this material has appeared in my "Tribute to Paula Gunn Allen (1939-2008)", Annette Van Dyke, *Studies in American Indian Literatures*, Series 2, Vol. 20, No. 4 (Winter 2008), pp. 68-75.

culture. Allen was born in Albuquerque, New Mexico, and grew up in Cubero, New Mexico, a Spanish-Mexican land grant village abutting the Laguna and Acoma reservations and the Cibola National Forest. She referred to herself as a "multicultural event," recalling her Pueblo, Lakota, Scottish ancestry from her mother, Ethel Haines Francis, and her Lebanese heritage from her father, Elias Lee Francis, a former lieutenant governor of New Mexico. These influences account for her ability to bridge perspectives and offer understandings across cultures, religions and worldviews.

She attended mission schools in Cubero and San Fidel, but was sent to a Sisters of Charity boarding school in Albuquerque from which she graduated in 1957. Her novel, *The Woman Who Owned the Shadows* (1983) and some of her poetry draws from this experience of being raised Catholic. However, Allen was well aware of the conflict that her background of being exposed to Catholic, Native American, Protestant, Jewish, and Marionite influences created. In an interview with Joseph Bruchac, Allen says: "Sometimes I get in a dialogue between what the Church taught me, the nuns taught me, and what my mother taught me, what my experience growing up where I grew up taught me. Often you can't reconcile them" (5).

Besides loss of respect, Ephanie, her main character in *The Woman Who Owned the Shadows*, must sort out the various influences that having a mixed ancestry brought in order to reclaim a Native American woman's spiritual tradition. On her journey, the protagonist uses traditional Laguna Pueblo healing ceremonies, as well as psychotherapy, the Iroquois story of Sky Woman, and the aid of a psychic EuroAmerican woman. *The Woman Who Owned the Shadows* is one of the first contemporary novels to have a complex Native American female as its central character and the first in which the main character's sexual orientation is primarily toward women. When questioned about the importance of balance between male and female in Native philosophy in regard to her character Ephanie, Allen explains, "For Ephanie to locate who she is, she has to move from thinking of her reference group as male to thinking of her reference group as female." She has to move into "[a] truly female universe." Her healing is reclaiming "her past, her place, and therefore her identity" and realizing she has "power in her own right" (Eysturoy 102-3).

Allen's poetry has an infusion of spirits common to Native American literature, but represents not only her Native American heritage, but also her multicultural heritage and lesbian orientation. The poem "Some Like Indians Endure" (*Life is a Fatal Disease* 147-50) compares the society's treatment of Native Americans to that of lesbians. "Beloved Women" explores the idea that in the ancient tribes "It is never known/if any woman was a Lesbian . . . /perhaps all women are/Lesbian . . . /perhaps all know the first/ beloved so well/they can shape the power/to reclaim her" (*Conditions* 65). This poem seems to echo the idea of a women's sphere in which women have their own power that has nothing to do with men.

Besides her essays collected in *The Sacred Hoop* and her own novel and poetry, Allen also promoted Native American women's spiritual writing in her collections of stories in *Spider Woman's Granddaughters: Traditional Tales and Contemporary Writing by Native American Women* (1989). She was particularly pleased with the reception of this last book that attempted to correct the lack of stories by and/or about Native women in the literature collections. She won the American Book Award for it from the Before Columbus Foundation in 1990. She also won the 1990 Native Prize for Literature. *In Grandmothers of the Light: A Medicine Woman's Sourcebook* (1991), Allen expanded her interest in the ritual experience of women as exhibited in the traditional stories. She traces the stages in a woman's spiritual path using Native American stories as models for walking in the sacred way.

In 2003, Allen's biography *Pocahontas: Medicine Woman, Spy, Entrepreneur, Diplomat* was published. Drawing upon her own Native background and her years of research, Allen continued her work on the centrality of women to Native cultures. Even in this last book, Allen explored the traditional spiritual roles of Native American women. She portrayed Pocahontas as a Beloved Woman who is in training to aid her Algonquin tribe with diplomacy dealing with the English settlers, demonstrating how the historical event of the "saving" of John Smith might be seen from a Native point of view.

In addition to her writings as critic, poet, novelist and scholar, Allen lived her spirituality, perhaps, demonstrating her idea of being a Native lesbian as a spiritual calling. Allen was an activist involved with such movements as antinuclear and anti-war, gay and lesbian, as well as feminist. She is especially well known on the West coast for her participation in gay and lesbian communities. In the mid-1980's, she served as associate fellow at the Stanford Humanities Institute, coordinating the Gynosophic Gathering, A Woman Identified Worship Service in Berkeley and giving weekly talks—"haggles"—at them.[4] Also, during this time, she was partners with the poet and essayist and another foremother in the area of women's spirituality, Judy Grahn, and is featured prominently in Grahn's *Another Mother Tongue: Gay Words, Gay Worlds* (1984). Grahn's philosophy behind her poetry was a particularly good match for Allen's in that she wrote from the "tribal traditions of

---

4 Three of these were published in *Trivia: A Journal of Ideas* 8 (Winter 1986) 61-73. She was also a contributor to a popular women's spirituality magazine, *Women of Power*. See, for instance, "The Woman I Love Is a Planet; The Planet I Love Is a Tree," 18 (Fall 1990): 5-7.

Northern Europe" creating poetry "that springs from a deep involvement with the earth as a real being" (Allen, "Judy Grahn" 7). This focus on earth as a real being and a female being at that, is a central idea of women's spirituality as a movement and as a discipline. Allen, of course, with her Native understanding of everything animate and inanimate having life and the centrality of women, has made enduring contributions to the intertwining fields of women's spirituality, lesbian studies, and women's studies. She has used her daring, original thinking to invent a whole new field of study and she will be remembered as a foremother who has passed on her legacy to the rest of us who follow.

"Bricolage" from the
Other End of the Continent

My No Conversations with Paula Gunn Allen

Márgara Averbach

Native U.S. Literature came to me magically, while I walked
down a Buenos Aires avenue and thought I was not looking
for it.

I was studying what it is now called African U.S. Literature as
part of a PhD course, and was browsing through the shelves of one
of the local bookstores that sell books in English when I came
across a writer I knew nothing about: Leslie Marmon Silko. I still
don't know why I bought the novel, but after I read *Ceremony*, I
could not stop reading—not just Silko, but also Linda Hogan,
Greg Sarris, Carter Revard, Louise Erdrich, Anita Endrezze,
Simon Ortiz, Paula Gunn Allen.

I read and read but I still think it was only when I read Paula
Gunn Allen's *The Sacred Hoop: Recovering the Feminine in American Indian Traditions*—I was already a PhD then—that I began to
understand a little more about Native U.S. Literatures, about the
different, alternative readings of the world that can be found in

them. But her book did quite a lot more for me: it even explained to me why I liked what Native U.S. authors had to say.

When I read *The Sacred Hoop*, I found a view of the world that was parallel (yet more coherent, more beautiful, wiser) to the one I had constructed as a child in my grandparents' *rancho* in Santa Fe, in the hot, dry North of Argentina (a *rancho* is a simple, straw-roofed house in the countryside; I keep the word in Spanish because "ranch" is a completely different thing in American English).

Just as is often the case with good literature and good criticism, *The Sacred Hoop* was the key to unexpected doors for me. Some of them were hidden in my own story, and that is why the core of Paula's book has become much more than just part of my classes, my bibliographies, my readings. I know I will never be able to read Native Literature the way Natives can. But for me, Paula's *Sacred Hoop* was the first thorough explanation of worldviews which could save the world as we know it. By the time I got to that book, I had been looking for that kind of explanation all my life.

I never met Paula, not even by e-mail, as I have Carter Revard, Simon Ortiz and Anita Endrezze. But some writers are the books they write, as José Saramago, the Portuguese Nobel Prize, once told me,[5] and Paula is one of them. My reading of her books and her articles has made her more than an acquaintance to me. I feel I have had "no conversations" with her, to paraphrase Louise Erdrich's *The Last Report on the Miracles at Little No Horse*.[6]

---

5 Averbach, Márgara. "*Yo quiero corregir la historia. Reportaje a José Saramago* (I want to correct History, Report to José Saramago)." *Cultura y Nación, Diario Clarín* January 26 1995.

6 Erdrich, Louise. *The Last Report on the Miracles in Little No Horse.* New York: Perennial, 2002.

These words—which I write in a language that is not my own and are therefore less poetic and less expressive than I would like them to be—are here to show the distance Paula's words can travel. As the swallows that come to Buenos Aires in September, our Spring, all the way from San Juan Capistrano, California, her words have the beauty and the strength necessary to get around the world and make summer possible.

Maybe that is why, when I read the conversation between John Purdy and Paula Gunn Allen, I felt like I could have been there listening and maybe saying something too. So here it is: a "no conversation" of three: Paula, John Purdy and me . . . from the other extreme of that continent we Latin Americans, call "América."

–\`⁄‵–

I was born in Buenos Aires, the biggest city in my country, but from three to six and every summer until I was ten, I lived in the North, with my grandparents, who were European city dwellers forced by fear and hunger into the movement called "*los gauchos judíos*," the Jew Gauchos. For me, our place, not too near a then very small town called Tostado was a sort of Paradise.

Now I know that my grandparents were not happy there. I knew it back then too, as children know almost everything, but it is only now that I can put that into words, now that my age (around fifty) allows me to remember with that kind of double consciousness typical of childhood memories, a consciousness which makes childhood an era when one is still a child and, at the same time, also an adult looking at what happens, interpreting it, understanding it in a different way, as in a science fiction time loop.

My grandparents were struggling in a world they did not really understand and it was a hard struggle. My parents did not have it easy either: every other weekend, they made a round-trip of around two thousand kilometers in a car a friend lent them to visit my brother and me. They were working eight hours a day in Buenos Aires and they did not want to leave us with anybody else. In the North, the weather was either too dry or too wet and always very hot. The place was full of serpents (some of them deadly) and pumas. The parrots and the wood pigeons ate the wheat seeds my grandfather was trying to plant. There was no electricity, no running water. I know now that my grandfather, my grandmother and my grand aunt—who lived with us—missed the city and hated everything around them.

I loved it.

I thrive in heat, even today. And in my family, kids were sacred: the grown-ups believed that they had to be happy and safe and that sadness should not touch them. Sadness did touch me, of course, but I felt I lived in Paradise. The world around me struck me as immensely beautiful. My grandfather taught me to read tracks, ride on horseback and fetch the cows and sheep when necessary.

Now I see that I was surprisingly independent in my ways to read the world, maybe because I had a feeling for everything around, even the serpents the adults were so afraid of. I interpreted what I saw in my own way.

Then, it was finished. My grandfather got very ill, we sold the place, brought him and my granny and aunt to live with us in our house, near Buenos Aires and never went back. I don't think anybody ever told me that we were leaving forever: I don't remember saying good-bye. From then on (I was twelve), I have lived here, in the suburb of Lomas de Zamora, and yet, my Northern past is still central in what I write, in the books I choose to work on, in what I like as a reader.

When I read *Ceremony* and then N. Scott Momaday's *House Made of Dawn*, I felt that those books spoke to me on a very deep level, deeper than anything I had read so far. But that does not mean I understood.

Only after reading *The Sacred Hoop* was I really able to enter these novels. When I got to Paula Gunn Allen, I was already looking for a guide. I understood that a large part of the Native U.S. novels I had read were completely out of my reach, and I knew why. I was separated from them by two degrees of culture—I am not a Native and I was not born in the U.S. or ever lived there more than a few months on end. Paula Gunn Allen's magic served to bridge that double gap.

I found the bridge again, firm and unshaken, when I read the conversation between Paula and John Purdy. I generally read aloud when I read something I am interested in. I remember doing that when reading their interview. I remember stopping from time to time and talking to the voices in the page. That is what I want to do here: I want to try and understand why certain sentences in the interview have a special brightness for me, a melody I recognize.

"I started doing criticism because nobody could read my work. Nobody could read Momaday's or anybody's, and so I started writing about it because there was no other way to get a readership."[7]

7 Purdy, John. "'And Then, Twenty Years Later . . .': A Conversation with Paula Gunn Allen." *Studies in American Indian Literatures* Fall 1997 5-16. Web Jan. 2009 http://www.hanksville.org/storytellers/paula/PGA-int.html.

Paula wanted readers. I wanted to be one of those readers. We were looking for each other. She really created a readership: Before I read *The Sacred Hoop*, I was miles from being part of it; after reading it, I think I can claim to belong to the group.

So these words are for me—for us, non-Native readers of Native Literatures. She guided us into the beauty and meaning and struggle of Native U.S. books, theater, pictures, movies and thought.

At the same time, she was also speaking to me as a critic (I work in a newspaper trying to say what I think about books): "Isn't that what every critic should do, create a readership for the books he or she loves?" she says. Yes, that is what a critic should do. Paula did and I am proof. I hope I am passing it on.

✵

"Everything has to be community, and it has to be multiple-community . . . "

Community is at the heart of Paula Gunn Allen's books, and is at the core of most Native U.S. Literature. That is another reason why I immediately liked her work. I have always looked for community stories as a reader and tried to write them as an author. There is, however, a difference between me and Native writers: I did not get to crave for community because of a communal experience—mine was a solitary family—but because of a lack of it. My parents talked about the need for community but they did not have it. That is maybe the reason why, when I write fiction, my books describe alliances and understandings, as is the case with *Una cuadra*,[8] my

8 Averbach, Márgara. *Una cuadra*. Buenos Aires: Adriana Hidalgo, 2008.

latest novel for adults, where a whole block groups together to paint images on the fronts of their houses.

When I read Paula Gunn Allen's *The Sacred Hoop* (and, much later, her *Studies in American Indian Literature: Critical Essays and Course Designs*),[9] I also understood that, while searching for community, I had written books which strangely erased the distinction between foreground and background, books without heroes. This probably explains why I, who am not a very good reader of theory, could not stop reading *The Sacred Hoop*, why I found it as enthralling as a novel.

"Because it's not binary, it's not either/or, and the thing is I would like to call the university a multiversity."

The understanding of the deep crack between European binary thinking and Native American non-binary worldviews (and here I am talking about the whole continent) was another gift I got from *The Sacred Hoop*. This is what Paula is talking about, I think, with that impressive formula which I read as "the university is a multiversity."

I had seen this idea in fiction books before I read Paula Gunn Allen's *Hoop*, but had not been fully able to understand it. I read more later in other critics, but Allen's words are the ones I remember. And those words took me back to the North of Santa Fe, where I had rejected the binary way of seeing things my elders passed on to me.

---

9 Allen, Paula Gunn. "Studies in American Indian Literature: Critical Essays and Course Designs," New York: MLA 1983. Print.; and *The Sacred Hoop: Recovering the Feminine in American Indian Traditions*. Boston: Beacon Press, 1986.

My family thought in binary pairs. My parents loved reading and taught me to read, and I owe them the universe of books. But they also loved and were very connected to European science. When we talked about something we called "Nature," we did not agree. They understood "Nature" within the binary pair "Human Beings versus Nature," where "human" was always positive and better than "Nature." My father, who was a doctor, considered medicine part of the fight *against* Nature and yet he was also a community man in more than one sense. That is another proof of the fact that things are more complex than binarism may lead us to think. He chose medicine in a country where physicians are very badly paid and he chose it not because he really liked it, but because his family needed a doctor. He was his family's doctor until he died. He used to have many patients who never paid because they could not pay. Yet he truly believed human beings were the center of the world and had the right to use and abuse animals, plants, rivers or mountains around them. He was already old when he started to change his views and I hope this change was because of me.

My grandparents were also constantly fighting Nature. It never occurred to them that they could fight *with* her. The war against parrots and wood pigeons is a good example of this. My grandfather saw them as enemies. I remember him with a long torch in his hand, trying to burn the big community nests that parrots had made in the tall eucalyptuses around the *rancho*. I hated him deeply for this. I think I almost remember the parrots in flames, but that may be an image I added later: after all, I was only five, six years old then, at most.

My grandfather saw Nature as his enemy, but again, sometimes he seemed to glimpse another way of understanding the world. One morning, he took me to the wheat fields on *Fosforito* (Little Match), the very tall *colorado* horse he generally rode. As soon as he put a foot on the ground, the wood pigeons, hundreds of them, took off from the recently sowed field. I remember being terrified. I thought I knew my grandfather and I was sure that he would be devastated by the vision of hundreds of birds eating his seeds. Sadness was common in my caring family and I was afraid of sadness. I remember looking down at him in fear (I was still on the horse). But he utterly surprised me: he was smiling.

"Isn't that a beautiful sound, Márgara?" he asked.

That day, he was my guide. He made me conscious of the noise of thousands of wings in the air, the impressive music of a community of wood pigeons rising to the hot skies all at the same time. I would not have noticed that without his smile. So sometimes he too saw beauty in Nature.

Today, I understand him: he had been taught the world one way and it was difficult for him to see it in any other. It is difficult for me too. I am still trying. I still need guides towards different possibilities.

And here's where Paula's books are important. They are all about possibility: among others, the possibility to write a different literature in English, to "reinvent the enemy's language," as Gloria Bird and Joy Harjo would say,[10] and to create a coherent, understanding readership.

Her books are not really about other books, they are about the world; I prefer books about the world. Paula Gunn Allen made me see how, in cultures where words are very close to what they name,

10 Harjo, Joy, and Gloria Bird (eds.). *Reinventing the Enemy's Language: Contemporary Native Women's Writings of North America.* New York: Norton, 1997.

language becomes a tool, a weapon to fight for what must be defended out of language: community, Earth, our relationship to others, not only human others but others in a more general, broader sense. I always wanted to do that with words.

There is yet another link I have with Paula: the problem of oral versus written language.

In the interview, Paula refers to the major role of oral tradition in Native U.S. cultures. Though I write, read, and live within a worldview where written and oral languages are opposite poles of a binary, and where written is considered better, more reliable and more important than oral, stories came first to me in the oral form.

When I was a child, I used to have frequent ear pains and there was only one way I could survive them: to have my mother read to me. She would read and I would listen, and if I listened carefully, at some moment, I would forget the pain completely. I have forgotten most of the stories but I do remember the joy of their infinite healing power. I have found that power in every book by Paula Gunn Allen I have ever read, including her critical works.

Later in life, when my family made long driving trips in summer—we drove from Buenos Aires to Salvador, Brazil, once; from Buenos Aires to Cuzco, Peru, another time; from Buenos Aires to Ushuaia, still other— mother (who never invented stories; that was not one of her gifts) went back to her habit of reading aloud. She sat in the front seat and read whole novels while we traveled. I did not want to arrive anywhere: traveling like that, in space and in imagination at the same time, was happiness to me. This became a family tradition: I read to my kids and my husband whenever we travel by car.

Reading like this, I have found out that only certain pieces of writing can be read aloud. The written language in Paula Gunn Allen prose, poetry, and essays translate easily into the human voice.

"There's no reason why we can't develop a contemporary Native American stance that enables us to generate political strategies that will apply. Not the same ones for everyone, but the appropriate ones for the case that you're examining."

Here we go again: "a university which is a multiversity."

I have always considered literature a very political phenomenon. And though Paula and I come from the two extremes of the continent, we are both on the same planet, and her criticism and literature are always *about* the planet, about the need to listen to the earth, to consider earth sacred. Maybe that is the reason Paula's words travel impressively far and sound impressively clear to people who, like me, believe that the center of our writings and lives should be the planet and the political fight for it.

She calls that idea "sacred;" I would probably call it something else, but I do share the feeling that it is the most important thing in the world today, the thing we should all write about.

"John Purdy: It's [the world views of Natives and non-Natives] fundamentally a very minor shift in one's point of view, but it's a world apart."

"PGA: It turns out to be major, and all you have to do is shift your eyes a little bit and suddenly you realize that wider pattern: it's the tree pattern, it's the hill pattern, it's the grass pattern, it's the literature discussion pattern . . . "

These words are about an alliance to save the planet and I want to belong to that alliance. But again, they speak to me in a personal way as well: "all you have to do is shift your eyes a little bit and suddenly you realize that wider pattern." That is what happened when my grandfather pointed to me the beauty of the sound of the pigeon wings in the wheat field.

Paula transmits these personal and political messages together and she shows us how to fight: by building a "university [that is] a multiversity" and making it strong, impossible to destroy.

We all live in this fragile house attacked by the terrible predators we, human beings, have become. Thank you, Paula, for making your bricolage tough and open and resistant and understandable to all: **"I'll tell you about my bricolage; I huffed and I puffed and I couldn't blow it down."**

Grandmother's Children & Grandchildren

Kristina Bitsue

Don't let them see you cry.
Don't let them hear you cry.
She struggled to live these years for so long.
And she lived them in beauty and happiness.

Don't let them see you cry.
Don't let them hear you cry.
Weeping by the fire at night
Won't bring her back.
But remember, the spirit of her lives forever.
Though in your heart is emptiness,
She shares her spirit with you.

Don't let them see you cry.
Don't let them hear you cry.
Into the dawning of tomorrow,
When father sun awakes,
Above and beneath you,
Her spirit will be there with you.
Her spirit lives forever.

We stood with her.
We shared stories with her.
We laughed with her.
We did everything we ever could with her.
But most of all, we loved her.

Don't let them see you cry.
Don't let them hear you cry.
She was all of our great, great grandmother.
The one who brought us to live.
The beauty of our life is from her.
Our teachings and learnings are from her.
Her spirit lives forever.

Don't let them see you cry.
Don't let them hear you cry.
For she will always be with you.
In my heart she tells me,
Tells me the days
When you would herd sheep and talk together.
Listen to the sky talk to you in the forest.
And watching you are all the spirits above.
'Till this day, they still are.

Dear mother,
Don't let them see you cry.
Don't let her see you cry.
Don't let them hear you cry.
Don't let her hear you cry.
The love she had for you was part of the strength in her heart.
She will miss you much.
But mother, dear mother, don't cry.
Remember her teachings.

The days in the woods you spent together.
The times you laughed together.
Remember she loved you a lot.
She is resting dear mother.
But at the same time she's loving you.
In her heart dear mother
Her love for you will never die.
Mother dearest,
Don't cry, be strong.
She lived in beauty for so long.
And where you look at *Chi Chil Tah-*
There she will be.

Why?
Because where you go,
Her spirit follows you with love.
And her home is a part of her.
So mother,
Even though it seems like she's not throwing her love at you.
Catch it anyway.
Don't cry, for her spirit is within . . .
Don't let her hear you cry.
For her spirit is within your heart.

And *shimasaani* (grandmother),
Even though I didn't say goodbye
When I greet the sun,
When I see the blue sky,
And when I meet the Navajo moonlight,
I know you will be there with me.

In the horizon I see two spirits dancing wildly,
with their wings spread freely

And their prayers answered;
I see the two spirits
Which I was created from.

Shimasaani doo shicheii (grandmother and grandfather),
I end this poem with goodbyes
and my love for you.

Time has passed.
We have accepted the fact that
You are resting in peace.

We cry no more,
But follow you happily
In your footsteps.

WE CARRY ON

Vintage Wagon
Kristina Bitsue

Long-Distance Gifts

For Paula Gunn Allen

(Originally published in *American Indian Culture &*
Research Journal, 2008)

Stephanie A. Sellers

Look into the palms of these hands
my hands were so young and inexperienced,
she took them gently, my teacher, my auntie
professor, my grandmother
the whole way from California
she took my hands into her hands
so she could look into the lines and
marks of my birth, my dreams, my
failures and joys. Into the depths of
what I brought with me through my
mother, what my ancestors, Natives
of the East and Jews from the Mediterranean
wrote on my hands, she read their messages.

All the way from California, Professor Auntie Paula
looked into my hands that she had taken
into her hands the month before, and declared

"Ah, you're a traditional."
"You better shake them up, girlfriend!"
"Jewish Indian women are dangerous, you know!"
Across the phone lines our voices travelled, from
sea to shining sea: half laughter and half Indian talk.
Across purple mountains' majesty: Laughing and culture
women's mixed blood laughter together with
women's mixed blood culture together with
women's mixed blood education together with
women's love. Mother and daughter. Teacher and student.
Grandmother of Ancient Wit and Tricks, and Granddaughter
learning the Women's Traditions written in eternity, caught among
college culture, blood politics, phone wires, and the last time we
    hugged.

Now I am standing under the white pine who has
cradled twenty-foot canes of pink rose blossoms
in my front yard. December's tornado pushed over
every oak in its path, but she still rises. My hands
are turned to the sky. It is June and
I am weeping at the loss of my treasured teacher
covered in fallen petals and honeysuckle perfume
in the dark I pray for her.

On Friday, with my hands still open I light
Sabbath candles and set a place for Auntie Paula
at our dinner meal. In a vase there are peony blossoms.
To the empty chair, to her spirit,
I tell jokes, then sit on the porch with my drum and sing.

For the White Lady Who Had Kokopelli's Statue Removed From a State Park

Deborah Miranda

It's a penis.
Your father has one.
Your brother has one.
Your son has one.
Your grandson has one.
It's a penis,
not the Mark of Cain.
It's a penis,
a prick,
a cock,
a dangler,
a clamdigger,
a babymaker,
a lovemaker,
a dick,
a dong,
a one-eyed snake
a pee pee
a wiener
a wankèr
but it's not

the Mark of Cain.
Your father has one.
Your son has one.
Hell, if you believe
in the Bible
God has one
(we are made
in His Image,
right?) I've got
news for you:
Indians
have 'em
too
or we wouldn't
still be
here
and maybe that's
your problem
with Mr. Kokopelli
and his joyful
manhood:
Indians having sex
means more Indians,
happy Indians,
straight
and gay,
mono or poly,
mixed or full.
Still here,
still happy:
is that too much
for you
to take?

Kopis'taya

Poets, Tricksters, Hollywood Indians & the Confluence of Paula Gunn Allen

Carolyn Dunn

Even so, the spirit voices are singing,
their thoughts are dancing in the dirty air.
Their feet touch the cement, the asphalt
delighting, still they weave dreams upon our
shadowed skulls, if we could listen.
If we could hear.

—Paula Gunn Allen
from *"Kopis'taya, a Gathering of Spirits"*

The presence of spirits in American Indian literature, the space between the spirit and secular worlds, and the borders and boundaries that inhabit these spaces have long been examined, in theory and practice, by Native and non-Native scholars alike. Paula Gunn Allen's groundbreaking work on matriarchal systems in Native cultures, *The Sacred Hoop: Recovering the Feminine in American Indian Traditions,* shifted the focus from the very male dominated Native activism of the 1970s and the male voice represented in Native literature, most notably in N. Scott Momaday's 1969 Pulitzer Prize winning novel *House Made of Dawn*, which had ushered in the Native American literary renaissance. The writings of Momaday, James Welch, and the spiritualist writings of Carlos Castaneda and Hyemeyohsts Storm (the latter two authors' authenticity was not questioned until many years later) left little room for Native peoples and communities whose "matriarchal, matrifocal, matrilineal, mother-right" societies were not recognized until Paula Gunn Allen turned her Ph.D. dissertation on her mother's and grandmother's stories into the recognition of the feminine in American Indian traditions that in 1986 were virtually unknown.

I, unlike Paula Gunn Allen, grew up in an urban area, nearly 2000 miles from my ancestral, tribal homelands. And like Gunn Allen, I grew up in a very matriarchal, matrifocal extended family who understood that men's roles and women's roles were not privileged one over the other, but have a shared equity that manifested itself in daily roles and rituals that complemented one another, in balance, in harmony; what the Navajo call Hozho: balance, walking in beauty. I grew up in Southern California, at a very young age participating in song, dance, and what I call local knowledge, that is the ceremonies and customs of the local California (Chumash, Tongva) Indians of Los Angeles.

I. [11]
I am the real Hollywood Indian,
born there on Sunset & Vermont in the heyday long before
Wounded Knee and Alcatraz and the movement
back when we were just "colored,"
and we tried on the Mestizo accent

[11] Carolyn Dunn, *"I Am The Real Hollywood Indian"*

of East Los,
and the signifying trait of Esu at the towers,
but later that voice became red and we spoke the language
of the colonizers
and we began to sing the songs of our own tongues cut out
by force from our mouths and red lines drawn in the blood
shell color of our ancestors
and I was that ancestor
on Sunset and Vermont.

My American Indian blood comes from the Creek, Cherokee, Seminole, Choctaw, and Tunica-Biloxi tribes of the southeast, from Oklahoma, Louisiana, Mississippi, North Carolina, South Carolina, and Alabama. My creative work has focused on the myths, legends, and ceremonial life of the ancestors and of the contemporary tribal life of my family, relatives, and friends. I grew up listening to the family stories and the creation stories of how we came to be, and how we traced our lineage all the way back to the Old Country: the Old Country being the old national, tribal boundaries and into the new nations after Removal. As I began my own journey as a poet, as a playwright, as a storyteller and a singer, learning from family and friends, I knew that as a second generation Californian, the Old Country to us was not another continent but a place that was just east of our modern homeland of Los Angeles, California. The stories of home became a lifeline for me, a connection to my immediate past and a connection to my ancestors who survived the unimaginable so that I could live. So, I began to write about what I knew of my family stories, with the knowledge that while I was an Indian from California, I wasn't a California Indian. I came from somewhere else.

II.

I am the real Hollywood Indian,
with my squash blossoms turning to silver butterflies in the breeze
in the old Los Angeles haze
and eagle vision spirit eye of the mountains at night,
the sparkle of city lights over a
haze of heat and desert air that causes me to breathe,
and I am flying
at night in the stars where I can see
through the eyes of the eagle,
Wahaliatka, Eagle Woman.

When I was seventeen, I left home and attended college at Humboldt State University, about 800 miles away from Los Angeles, in California's Redwood Forest. Ninety-five miles from the Oregon border, it is the home of several American Indian tribes including the Wiyot, Yurok, Karuk, Hupa and Tolowa tribes. I was invited to ceremonies and into family gatherings of folks who belonged to those tribes. But the longing I experienced, the longing for a place and for a people I had no physical connections too, was strong. I felt lost, adrift, away from home and family, embraced by a community that although welcomed and continues to welcome me, wasn't my knowledge. And then I met Paula Gunn Allen.

III.

I am the real Hollywood Indian,
not some Miss Thang turned California golden child,
sniffing the remnants of some china cup and saucer
thrown to the night wolves along Sunset and Gower –
their studio is my front yard and

I act out desires on flesh and blood,
red lines on paper, tea and scones at sundown,
boy of the moment no longer and I am more real than you will ever
know.

Paula Gunn Allen's influence upon me, personally and professionally, began in 1986 when she was doing a book tour for her groundbreaking book, *The Sacred Hoop: Recovering the Feminine in American Indian Traditions.* I was the host of a public affairs news radio program in Arcata, California called *Native Voices,* and I interviewed Paula in the home of the show's producer, Irena Quitiquit. Coming from the Laguna Pueblo perspective, a tribe which had been, like my own, matrilineal and matrilocal, her assertion that the feminine principle in American Indian cultures had long been ignored resonated with me as a then twenty-year-old Indian woman from Los Angeles, living in the diaspora of Northern California, where I was very active in the local community.

Paula gave me a signed copy of her novel *The Woman Who Owned the Shadows* (Spinsters Ink/Aunt Lute Books, 1983) and I would later say that the novel saved my life. Six years later, while at graduate school in the American Indian Studies program at UCLA, my thesis chair Kenneth Lincoln suggested I work with Paula, who would be coming from UC Berkeley to join UCLA's English department. I was her research assistant for two years and she was a member of my thesis committee. We formed a close bond that would remain for the rest of her life. She promoted my work as a scholar and as a poet, publishing my first book of poetry in 2001 and continuing to support me artistically and academically. I was honored to have been asked to sing at her funeral by her daughter, Lauralee Brown Hannes and her son,

Sulieman Russell Allen, to send her on her journey home. To say that she influenced me personally, professionally, and politically is a great understatement.

When we met, I had just turned 21, and was graduating from college. I always loved, years later, telling that story, because although Paula would always say "I met CD when she was a young undergrad and she interviewed me on a small, public radio show and asked me the best questions about a book she had never read," the irony of that story was that while yes, I did not read the novel Paula had published two years earlier, *The Woman Who Owned The Shadows*, nor had I read the book of essays she was promoting, *The Sacred Hoop*, she did not remember even meeting me nor being interviewed by me on that late winter day in 1986! She would only find out, a few short years later, that that moment changed my life and set me on course that I would follow, in her footsteps still today. I received those two books that day and I opened up *The Woman Who Owned the Shadows* when I got home and began to read,

> In the beginning was Spider. She divided the world. She made it. Thinking, thus she made the world. She drew lines that crossed each other. Thus were the directions. Thus were the powers. Thus were the quadrants. Thus the sol-stices. Thus were the seasons. Thus was the woman. Within these lines she placed the two small medicine bundles. Sing-ing, she placed them. In the sacred way she placed them. In the sacred way she played them. There were no others then but the Spider who sang. [12]

---

12 *The Woman Who Owned the Shadows*, Spinsters Ink/Aunt Lute Books, San Francisco. 1st edition, 1983.

The story of Ephanie Atencio is about a mixed blood American Indian woman recovering from a nervous breakdown brought on by years of abuse, an identity crisis, and how she brings the pieces of her broken self back together by returning to the ancestral stories of her mother and grandmother and the "universe of medicine." Ephanie's story spoke to me as a mixed blood Native woman living in the Redwood Forest, doubly removed from home and family; triple removed if you counted the original Removal on the Trail of Tears and the subsequent survival by intermarrying and creating a whole new Indigenous culture that merged the strands of Indian, European, and African to make the Creole people.

The theme of the universe of medicine is a connecting thread that carries through diaspora, home, storytelling, humor, healing, and sovereignty, and that ties these concepts to the larger issue of nation-building and narrative-within-national boundaries that ghost my own work as a poet, playwright, singer, and mother. This narrative thread was first woven by Grandmother Spider, nurtured by a strong line of powerful women: my mother, aunts, grandmothers, and my beloved mentor, Paula Gunn Allen. She encouraged me to write my family stories, and she understood where they came from. Like me, she was an Indian living in California who wasn't a California Indian.

IV.
I am the real Hollywood Indian,
a blessing and burden of myth,
a howl on a night wind, vision and virgin light from the dead
stars above,
down through the canyons loping with a bay moon of time and
space and all that is between

and I am still here,
Watching creation spin on its axis and spitting out the stars

The metaphor of the Sacred Fire is the method with which I have entered into the conversations of what it means to be a modern Creek and Cherokee Indian in the world today. It is also a metaphor that I have utilized in my academic work, that is, the study of how poets and storytellers write about "home," especially those connections between landscapes that normally may not have a connection to one another, other than they are inhabited and stewarded by Indigenous peoples. The Sacred Fire connects the Creek, Cherokee, Choctaw, Seminole, Yuchi, Chickasaw peoples of contemporary southeastern U.S. to the ancestral landscape from which we emerged: modern day Alabama, Georgia, Tennessee, North Carolina. The Sacred Fire traveled with the ancestors to Indian Territory, now Oklahoma. Along with the Sacred Fire traveled the stories of its emergence and appearance on the earth.

Our ancestral stories tell us that Grandmother Spider, the water spider who can travel over water safely and quickly, brought back the fire from the sun so that the world would no longer be cold. From this Sacred Fire that Grandmother Spider brought, ceremonial fires are lit for the coming year and the fire that Grandmother Spider brought has never gone out. It is through the fire that we trace our ancestry to the origins of the world, from the emergence of the mounds to the red earth of Indian Territory, Oklahoma, to the modern nations that have emerged after years of dispossession, theft, loss, and grief. The fire was carried on the Trail of Tears by our ancestors and that fire has never gone out, that fire that came from the sun. This is the metaphor that teaches us continuance and survivance, and it is from these fires that we warm our homes and ceremonial grounds. It is from these fires that we make our worlds through story, poem, song, and dance.

I surrounded myself with other Indians from other places, and when I met family and friends from home, it was as if we had never been apart. So, in an attempt to understand why I do what I do in my own creative work, I began to look at other Creek, Cherokee, Choctaw and Seminole artists who, like me, had a connection to a homeland that was part of the American south. What were/are the similarities in our work? What are the questions of southeastern American Indian identity that surface through our creative lives? What do our poems, stories, songs, plays say about the world in which we live in—that is the home world where we live (the local) and the home world from where we emerged (the national)? What are, as Karuk scholar/storyteller/ musician Julian Lang calls them, local knowledges, and how do they relate to national knowledges?

Still, I was in Los Angeles. Los Angeles boasts the largest urban American Indian population in the United States. With nearly 300,000 American Indians residing in the city, Los Angeles remains a city of disjointed gathering places for Indians. Those who come to the city tend to gather around cultural events such as pow wows, theater events, and church groups, the latter especially true for southeastern Indians. Joan Weibel Orlando notes in Indian Country, L.A., that northern plains tribes will congregate around pow wows and at the Southern California Indian Center, while southern Indians tend to gather around monthly sings, where folks gather to sing Baptist hymns in the Creek, Choctaw, or Cherokee languages. Community building among the Indians of Los Angeles, Weibel-Orlando posits, has been a kind of cultural patchwork, a bricolage, a highly creative and dynamic endeavor. The bricolage of which Weibel-Orlando refers to comes from Claude Levi-Strauss' process of building something from older sociocultural forms. Methods of building community in Los Angeles among the diversity of its American Indian citizens has certain challenges of space and landscape that preclude there being an actual physical space, or city center, which lends itself to building an Indian community in a central location. American Indian community building revolves around events, such as pow wows, and other intertribal events. Rarely will members of the larger American Indian community gather at the sacred or ceremonial sites of the local tribes, the Chumash or the Tongva, for example, for Chumash or Tongva ceremonies. I have observed on many occasions this handful of non- Tongva or Chumash citizens, and in general these small groups of non-Tongva and Chumash—that is Indians from California that are not California Indians—tend to be those who are involved in pan-tribalism on a cultural literacy level. These are the storytellers, the language revitalizationists, the environmental activists who are actively engaging with the local communities in Los Angeles, all the while maintaining connections to their ancestral tribes and homelands.

V.

I am the real Hollywood Indian,
the one who left and remained the same,
who emerged from dark desert canyons and minds of frightened girls,
who lived to tell the tale and keeps telling,
shouting out blood to all who will listen,
spitting red on a page to all who will hear
and I am still here.

Chumash storyteller, poet, and Professor Georgiana Valoyce-Sanchez and I produced the radio program for KPFK-FM's American Indian Airwaves/Coyote Radio in which we examined cultural literacy in American Indian communities in Los Angeles. For the program we interviewed Julian Lang, Cheryl Seidner, and Arigon Starr as to what every Indian, and every non-Indian, should know about not only their own culture, but the culture of the Indigenous people whose space and place they inhabit. "There's local knowledge," Julian Lang answered, "and that is how one interacts with one's environment. The local knowledge of the local people, their language, ceremonies, songs and dances, is what everyone should know, in addition to their own." This concept remains with me today, five years later, and a concept that I have practiced in my years as an Indian who is from California, but not a California Indian. Indians who have that connection then to a local landscape, as well as a home landscape, traverse a bicultural Native landscape that is inclusive of other languages, cultures and religions outside of their own. These American Indians live in a diaspora within national boundaries, a diaspora that is, like many Native landscapes, a nation within a nation.

As I further investigated the concept of local knowledge and national knowledge, I began my quest to define and establish the definition of a diaspora within national borders. As American Indians, we are a people of national and ethnic origin that live within the boundaries of another nation-state, a nation-state that continues to oppress and deny our right to sovereign status as self-governing bodies. While diaspora studies scholars focus on international borders and dialogues of nation to nation dispersal, we, as American Indians, remain dispersed peoples within the boundaries of our ancestral homelands. I have learned songs in many languages as a singer, in Blackfoot, Lakota, Paiute, Towa

(Jemez Pueblo), Wintu, Ojibwe and Cree. I have made songs in Choctaw and Creek, and passed those songs onto others. As American Indians, our languages and religions and ceremonies encompass over five hundred distinct nations and groups, yet we reside within a specific national border. The sharing of local and national knowledges, that is the sharing of Indigenous epistemologies, is as fluid and ever-changing as it ever was, when communities came together because of dispersal and diasporization in the old nations as well as in the new ones. The diversity of Indian Country could represent its own mini United Nations. This was the context in which I met, interviewed, and was gifted with mentoring by Paula Gunn Allen.

In my work, this work that is so influenced by Paula Gunn Allen, I examine the notion that Native peoples in the United States, those involved with local communities as well as communities back home, are bicultural in the sense that Solomona and other Maori living in Aboriginal communities in Australia experience. I examine theories of bicultural competence, something that was introduced to me at a conference in New Zealand by Maori social worker Roseanna Henare Solomona, living in Queensland, Australia and working in both a Maori and Aboriginal community. American Indians in the diaspora, those involved with local communities as well as communities back home, are bicultural in the sense that like Solomona and other Maori living in Aboriginal communities in Australia, experience both the stories, songs and ceremonies of local communities as well as those back home. The sharing of songs, stories, and ceremony not as commodity but as cultural history is what prompted me to first investigate, as a project, Indigenous epistemologies that interact with one another on the sociocultural level. The actual term that I am in conversation with bicultural comes from Solomona's research, and she describes it as such:

Nonetheless I stand firm in my decision to put pen to paper in this fashion, purely because this work is written for Maori who have not enjoyed the privilege of a traditional upbringing, especially those who have lived away from the language, the people and the culture. This mahi or work is for the new generation of Maori, half-castes, quarter-castes or those who left the homeland as children. They are our young contemporaries who have been raised knowing they inherit a rich tradition, yet understand very little about it. It is also for Maori who remain on the fringes of our culture and who stand as a reminder of our colonial past, a generation who longs to reconnect with their Maoritanga. Finally it is for those people for whom we share this country with, first nation people and multicultural Australia.[13]

In describing the tribal culture in which she was raised, Solomona is returning to her traditions to share them with those who were not raised as she was, attending ceremony, an event that connected her to the ancestral political, cultural, linguistic, and spiritual foundations of her Maori (Ngatihine and Ngapuhi) identity.

In an attempt to reach across cultures—Maori, English, Aboriginal— Solomona describes the actual writing of her thesis as a multicultural event. The term bicultural to me is not representative of a duality in terms, e.g. white/Indian, black/Indian, black/ white, but the concept that Native peoples are schooled in duality since birth in the United States. Duality comes from the understanding of a fluency in cultures; there is a dualism that must be negotiated for Native peoples that I have expressed

13 Roseanna Henare Solomona, "Whakaaro-rua: A Bicompetent Approach to Inquiry. Honors Thesis," University of Western Sydney, Australia. 2004. p 28.

as bicultural rather than multicultural or multi-literate. I favor Solomona's term because it expresses the dual nature or function of cultures within the Native consciousness that is always present for Native peoples, whether in the Indian world only, or the non-Indian world. Bicultural, or bicompetent, reflects the constant nature of negotiating between worlds, a state in which Indigenous people around the world must constantly traverse.

VI.
I am the real Hollywood Indian,
a ceremony in the making.
On Sunset and Vermont running on all fours,
a hat of black velvet covering my youth, my blessed age,
my being and continuing that is the song of my mother,
and I will not tell you again,
my words have been spoken.

The bicultural literacy that many Indigenous peoples comprehend is how I would describe what Paula Gunn Allen spent considerable time on in her academic and creative work referring to the universe of medicine, that is the collective and creative unconscious of tribal peoples in the Americas. In her introduction to *Spider Woman's Granddaughters: Traditional Tales and Contemporary Writing by Native American Women*, Gunn Allen describes the universe of medicine:

Native writers write out of tribal traditions, and into them. They, like oral storytellers, work within a literary tradition that is at base connected to the ritual and beyond that to tribal metaphysics or mysticism. What has been experienced over the ages mystically and communally—with individual experiences fitting within that overarching pattern—forms the basis for tribal aesthetics and therefore tribal literatures.[14]

The communal experience of tribal reality is, at the core, what comprises an essential connection to the tribal worldview. Storytellers reference the tribal aesthetic and modern literary writers, tapping into the traditional story, are referencing ages of experience and Indigenous epistemologies. Indigenous knowledge, or ways of learning and knowing, are replicated in the story over and over, in performance, in practice, and now, in theory. In Native epistemologies, in Native realities, the practice comes first before the theory. This is what I spend considerable amount of time addressing.

The term American Indian identity is problematic, at best. A socially constructed ethnic identity in the United States and abroad, the term American Indian (and later, Native American) signified a unified racial category to describe thousands of peoples of varying languages, cultures, religions, and world views. Of all racial categories in the United States, only one racial category is defined legally and enforced by the federal government; that is the racial category: American Indian. The essentializing strategies employed by the federal government to divide and conquer the tribal power of the Indigenous peoples inhabiting the United States created further legislation, which allowed the federal government to forcibly remove tribal peoples from their ancestral homelands into urban areas with promises of jobs and security. Urban relocation in the 1950s and 1960s was the culmination of a series of government policies designed to assimilate Indians into mainstream culture, isolating Indian families and

14 Paula Gunn Allen. *Spider Woman's Granddaughters*, p 9.

communities. However, tribal peoples continued to make connections with one another in urban areas and created a network
of community that would later give birth to the pan-Indian
movement. For the Native diaspora, the pan-Indian movement
allowed for a creation of communal space in urban areas in
which an urban Indian identity flourished. Community centers,
pow-wows, and urban health clinics became the places in which
Native peoples congregated and shared stories of home: the
ancestral home left behind as well as the adopted urban home.
Cultural production that came out of urban areas, such as
Spiderwoman Theatre and American Indian Theatre Project in
New York, addressed the concerns affecting the Native diaspora. Novelists and poets explored questions of identity and
authenticity, writing on subjects of alienation, loss, and survival
in urban areas, with an abject longing for home. I have examined
responses of Native artists to the following questions: Once
removed from the ancestral landscape, how does the longing for
home create community in new spaces? As home becomes a
memory to an intergenerational diaspora, how is home a created
space? How is nation building achieved by tribes whose members are scattered diasporically? How do artists incorporate the
idea of home into their work? Are there multiple sites of home,
of community, and of nation?

Where do these spaces, both imagined (as a contested site of
removal, of resistance, of domestication) and physical (as a place
of emergence and connectedness to its physical boundaries),
occur in the imagination of the artist? How must the Native
artist navigate within nations, with an eye to the home nation,
and with respect and responsibility to the local nation? And
finally, in seeking out other Natives and living among Native
communities who still live in their ancestral homelands, how

does home become both spaces, the diasporic as well as the ancestral? This is the cultural context of Native literatures.

Paula Gunn Allen argued in 1986 that in order to understand cultural contexts within tribal literary and performative practices, one must have an understanding of the cultural aesthetic from which the literature arises:

> Literature is one facet of a culture. The significance of a literature can be best understood in terms of the culture from which it springs and the purpose of the literature is clear only when the reader understands and accepts the assumptions on which the literature is based. A person who was raised in a given culture has no problem seeing the relevance, the level of complexity, or the symbolic significance of that culture's literature. We are all from early childhood familiar with the assumptions that underlie our own culture and its literature and art. Intelligent analysis becomes a matter of identifying smaller assumptions peculiar to the locale, idiom, and psyche of the writer.[15]

The cultural aesthetic follows logical assumptions that in studying national literatures that one must look to the culture from which these literatures arise. Cultural touchstones, for example, are imperative in understanding the great canonical works of western literature.

Do literary critics and scholars assume knowledge of western thought and practice when it comes to understanding the great canonical works? The assumption is that western epistemology

---

15 Paula Gunn Allen, *The Sacred Hoop.* p 54.

is a given in this context, but to study Native literatures using a non-Native aesthetic makes no sense in examining the works of Native peoples. Yet the practice of employing western assumptions and a western aesthetic to Native knowledges is a colonial practice that Linda Tuhiwai Smith argues must be acknowledged and addressed if scholars are to decolonize the study of Native peoples and bring cultural context into American Indian history.

VII.
I am the real Hollywood Indian,
speechless and serene in my rage
and I will scream at the top of my voice
until I can no longer force it back up,
birthing stars and dreaming the Sun,
new visions and new ceremonies
and I will call you home.

To understand Native aesthetics, one must understand Native ethics. As I have noted, "… there is no division between the sacred world of spirits, deities, myth, ritual, and cosmology and the secular world of political structure, economics, family life, and personal life. Our religion, our culture, and our traditions are seamlessly woven together and cannot be separated. Our religions are part of our social lives, and our social lives are connected to our spirituality."[16]

16 Carolyn Dunn, "The Trick is Going Home: Secular Spiritualism in Native American Women's Literature," Reading Native American Women: Critical/creative Representations, ed. Ines Hernandez-Avila, AltaMira Press, 2005.

We must address spiritualism, myth, and the presence of archetypal tribal spirits in American Indian writing. There is indeed an acknowledged spiritual presence in American Indian poetry and prose. Chickasaw writer and poet Linda Hogan describes the presence of such spirits in her work:

> As my interest in literature increased, I realized I had also been given a background in oral literature from my father's family. I use this. It has strengthened my imagination. I find that my ideas and even my work arrangement derive from that oral source. It is sometimes as though I hear those voices when I am in the process of writing.[17]

The concept of tribal consciousness becomes important while studying spiritualism and myth in American Indian literature, and the concept of tribal aesthetics, as defined by Gunn Allen in *Spider Woman's Granddaughters*, shows the reader and critic alike the collective vision of Indian peoples. The Western Euro-American critic first must be aware of the tribal concept of aesthetics when discussing American Indian literature. What motivates the Indian writer is not the sense of self and individuality, but working for goals that are common within the community. It is a shared consciousness, working for the whole of the community rather than the whole of the self. Analytical work has been done on the trickster figure in American Indian mythology. This is where Carl Gustav Jung's ideas of tribal consciousness combined with Gunn Allen's concept of tribal aesthetics becomes important. In his essay "The Trickster" from *Four Archetypes*, Jung discusses tribal consciousness: "It is a personification of traits of a character which are sometimes worse

---

17 Interview with Linda Hogan, 1985, conducted and transcribed by Laura Coltelli, *Winged Words: American Indian Writers Speak* (University of Nebraska Press, 1990). p 71.

and sometimes better than those the ego personality possesses. A collective personification, like the Trickster, is a product of an aggregate of individual as something known to him, which would not be the case if it were just an individual outgrowth."[18]

Jung's work, like Gunn Allen's, focuses on tribal beliefs, which she sees as of value to the community as a whole rather than to the individual as an isolate entity. Gunn Allen writes in her introduction to *Spider Woman's Granddaughters*, "The aesthetic imperative requires that new experiences be woven into existing traditions in order for personal experience to be transmuted into communal experience, that is, so we can understand how today's events harmonize within the communal experience . . . We use aesthetics to make our lives whole, to explain ourselves to each other, to see where we fit into the scheme of things."[19]

Following our own aesthetic becomes vital when looking to our own traditional cultures for illumination and contextualization of our own canon. Our world shifts between the sacred and the secular effortlessly yet without ease; in this duality of life, we become the trickster figure within our own context.

VIII.
I am the real Hollywood Indian,
the trickster who birthed herself,
Wahalitka, Eagle Woman,
sharp-eyed, fierce-lipped,
denied everything, given nothing

18 Carl Gustav, *Four Archetypes: Mother / Rebirth / Spirit / Trickster.* Bollingen Series, Princeton University Press. p 71.

19 Paula Gunn Allen. *Spider Woman's Granddaughters*, p 7.

save for the hawk at my back,
the thorn in my side,
silver butterflies visioning heaven,
caustic vision and ancestral memory in the eye of the eagle,
and I will see you reborn.

Paula Gunn Allen, in her creative and scholarly work, was indeed the trickster figure in her own work, the Hollywood Indian living at the corner of Sunset Boulevard and Vermont Avenue, in the shadows of the mythical world of the imagined Indian, staring in the face the fully realized, bicultural, bicompetent experience and lived experience of a mother right, matrilineal, matrifocal, diasporic mixed blood Laguna Pueblo Indian hundreds of miles from home in Los Angeles. Those of us who knew her, and those who look to her work and continue her legacy of landscape, a universe of medicine, trickster methodology, and recovering the feminine in traditions honor her memory and keep her with us at every sacred fire we carry with us.

Seeing Through Native Eyes

Paula Gunn Allen's Writing as Ritual & Prophecy

Jennifer Browdy

Paula Gunn Allen's two major collections, *The Sacred Hoop: Recovering the Feminine in American Indian Traditions* and *Grandmothers of the Light: A Medicine Woman's Sourcebook*, can be read as visionary repositories of myth and ritual in the Native American gynocentric tradition, providing blueprints for contemporary activists, Natives and non-Natives alike, who seek to help bring human society and planet Earth into better alignment for a sustainable future.

Paula Gunn Allen died on May 29, 2008, at the age of 68. Two years earlier, already sick with asthma, emphysema and the beginnings of the lung cancer that would take her life, she survived a devastating fire, which destroyed her trailer home. In the aftermath of that traumatic episode, she wrote an open letter to her friends, in which she led into her vivid description of the night of the fire by talking about her mother's recent passing:

> I didn't know what I'd do without her [my mother], because I
> knew the only reason I had been able to go out into the world and
> do the things I had done, good, bad, and indifferent, professional,
> personal, spiritual, was that she was there, home, keeping the fire

alight, tending to the world in a quiet way that appeared to be cooking, cleaning, ordering a human family's life.

Last night I was again faced with the dilemma. I am not old. I am not wise. I am not a protector. I have no one to ask how to do something, what to do, someone who I just know is there holding the world together. It can't be me ... I'm too small, too vulnerable, too ignorant. But the ones who do know, who are older and wiser, are all gone.

From this admission of vulnerability Allen goes on to describe in clear, painful detail what happened later that night, when some rags caught fire in her shed and the flames spread to the trailer. Wheezing and gasping, she called 911, and was rushed from the scene in an ambulance, oxygen and nebulizer humming. Her house burned down, but she was safe, and she ends her letter on a typically positive note, remembering how later, when it was all over,

I was leaning on the trunk resting my aching back ... or excruciating hip, or both ... and happened to look down. I saw my left hand and a warm feeling of aesthetic pleasure washed through me. Gee, I thought, I have pretty hands. For the most part I haven't liked my hands, but that day their brownness, their strength, the length of my fingers, the raised veins ... wow. Then in a flash I was elsewhere, and a fresh small breeze was moving through me, or WAS me, and as images of the blackened remains of my past flicked by I grokked: "Yikes! I flashed. I've been believing that was real!" (and of course it's not, the unverbalized remainder of the grok continued). YAHOO! How I wish that nice feeling would stay. But how grateful I am that I had a moment's clarity, freedom, objective awareness. That was what the fire etc is/was all about, after all. You friend-warriors know what I mean.[20]

20 Paula Gunn Allen, "The Perils of Being—3"

Interestingly, Allen's apprehension that there was spiritual meaning in the fire incident beyond the obvious loss of her home sprang from the very material realities of her "aching back," "excruciating hip," and her strong brown hands. The physical realm (the body, in this case) brings pain, but also prompts the transformation of pain into story, and Allen's stories, drawn from tribal traditions and history as well as from her own experience, are always about resistance, empowerment and healing, especially of, by and for women.

Although she may not have realized it, by the time of her 2006 fire after the death of her own mother, she was passing from "the Way of the Teacher" to "the Way of the Wise Woman," a traditional Native woman's journey that she chronicled in her 1991 volume *Grandmothers of the Light: A Medicine Woman's Sourcebook*. Such transitions are never easy, and always accompanied by pain, she wrote. "Those who essay to walk the medicine path hoping for a more pleasurable existence are bound to be disappointed. Each increment of power one gains along the path of power requires sacrifice and exacts its toll of suffering and pain. In the universe of power everything has its price." The practitioner "must be disciplined and committed enough to follow the requirements of her path regardless of the pain it causes her (*Grandmothers* 13). Always the teacher, Allen shared her own experience of the painful but enlightening fire and its aftermath with a wide audience, allowing herself to "serve as a model for younger women on the path [so that] her presence, her essence, [would] enter into the life of the community to enrich and revitalize it" (*Grandmothers* 14).

In *The Sacred Hoop* Allen obliquely acknowledges her own shamanic practice, admitting that her work is strengthened by "guidance from the nonphysicals and the supernaturals . . . I am especially fortunate because the wind and the sky, the trees and the rocks, and the sticks and the stars are usually in a teaching mood; so when I need an answer to some dilemma, I can generally get one. For which I must say thank you to them all" (*Sacred Hoop* 7). Shamanic practice as Allen defines it uses storytelling and ritual to bring balance, harmony and healing to the world. "Myth and ritual are the wings of the bird of spirit," Allen says. "The one contains knowledge of language while the other embodies that knowledge in action. Myth, you might say, is noun, while ritual is verb. Myth is weft, ritual is woof. The true shaman weaves them together in harmony with all that is to create a tapestry that furthers wholeness and enriches life for all beings" (*Grandmothers* 8).

Allen's writing both draws on myth and ritual and enacts them; out of the scattered and sometimes tattered threads of Native American cultural traditions from across North America and as far south as Central America, she weaves a vivid and powerful new story, centered on, as the subtitle to *The Sacred Hoop* makes clear, "recovering the feminine in American Indian traditions." Realizing that women's contributions to Native culture had been systematically erased by the patriarchal lens through which the tribes were viewed from the earliest days of European contact right up into the 20th century, Allen made women's traditions the focus of her scholarly work. She recognized that while "American Indian women's traditions are largely about continuity . . . men's traditions are about transitoriness or change. Thus, women's rituals and lore center on birth, death, food, householding and medicine (in the medical rather than the magical sense of the term)—that is, all that goes into the maintenance of life over the long term. Men's rituals are concerned with risk, death, and transformation—that is, all that helps regulate and control change" (*Sacred Hoop* 82).

Both feminine and the masculine traditions and practices are necessary for a balanced, harmonious society, Allen says, but as a woman, her particular focus throughout her career was on the feminine side, which she saw as having special value for the survival and strengthening of Native peoples.

When we shift our attention from the male, the transitory, to the female, the enduring, we realize that the Indians are not doomed to extinction but rather are fated to endure. What a redemptive, empowering realization this is! As the Cheyenne have long insisted, no people is broken until the heart of its women is on the ground. Then they are broken. Then they will die (*Sacred Hoop* 267).

Allen was at the forefront of a chorus of contemporary Native American women writers insisting on the vibrancy of their hearts and lives, and on their ability to heal pain through the transformative power of storytelling and myth. As Chicana/*mestiza* writer/activist Gloria Anzaldua noted, "It was through writing that the Conquest was enacted" by the Europeans, inscribing a new story on the backs of the Native peoples so strongly that in some cases, they began to believe it themselves. Nevertheless, they survived, following their own forms of resistance: "American Indians . . . have more often than not refused to engage in protest in their politics as in their fiction and poetry," Allen says. "They have chosen rather to focus on their own customs and traditions and to ignore the white man as much as possible. As a result, they have been able to resist effectively both colonization and genocide" (*Sacred Hoop* 82). Native American women writers, "*mestizas* and Native women who use the pen—or should I say the keyboard—as a weapon and a means of transformation," Anzaldua says, are "reclaiming the agency of reinscribing, taking off [the colonizers'] inscriptions and reinscribing ourselves, our own identities, our own cultures. The very weapon that conquered Indigenous America, we're using it against them" (*Interviews* 189).

Allen chose to wield the weapon of writing not so much *against* the dominant American society, but rather as a teacher, patiently seeking to educate the American mainstream, including scholarly specialists in the fields of anthropology and literary studies, to see the feminine side of Native American traditional and contemporary literature more clearly. The aim of her teaching was not simply academic, but also frankly activist. "Traditional tribal lifestyles are more often gynocratic than not, and they are never patriarchal," she maintained. Gynocentric tribal societies "are focused on social responsibility rather than on privilege," and they "feature even distribution of goods among all members of the society ... Among gynocratic or gynocentric tribal peoples the welfare of the young is paramount, the complementary nature of all life forms is stressed, and the centrality of powerful women to social well-bring is unquestioned" (*Sacred Hoop* 2-3). Allen maintained that the study of gynocentric tribal societies was important not just in its own right, but also because such societies can provide important models for contemporary activists who seek to bring about positive social change. Understanding gynocentric tribal cultures is "essential to all responsible activists who seek life-affirming social change that can result in a real decrease in human and planetary destruction and in a real increase in quality of life for all inhabitants of planet earth," she said (Sacred Hoop 2).

For Allen, as for many Native writer/activists, both writing and activism are deeply spiritual acts. Native writers, Allen says, need not "choose between spirituality and political commitment, for each is the complement of the other. They are the two wings of one bird, and that bird is the knowledge of the interconnectedness of everything (*Sacred Hoop* 169). This vision of "the interconnectedness of everything" informs and animates all of Allen's writing. Despite her acknowledgement that Native peoples have often chosen to "ignore the white man," this was not her path. A *mestiza* herself, of Laguna/Keres and Lebanese descent, Allen always writes to share her insights and visions with a broad, inclusive audience, both Native and non-Native. "Vision is a way of becoming whole," she says, "of affirming one's special place in the universe . . . The vision . . . as vision can be experienced only by one person directly. Yet it, like all aspects of Indian life, must be shared; thus myth. Myth is the story of a vision . . . it is a vehicle of transmission, of sharing, of renewal, and as such plays an integral part in the ongoing psychic life of a people, (*Sacred Hoop* 116).

Much of Allen's written work consists of retellings of traditional stories and myths, which she relates with the intention of giving contemporary women, both Native and non-Native, the tools to keep their own hearts, and the hearts of their peoples, off of the ground.

> The question that American Indian writers face again and again . . . is this: How does one survive in face of collective death? Bearing witness is one solution, but it is singularly tearing, for witnessing genocide . . . requires that someone listen and comprehend. . . . Audiences for the American Indian writer . . . are sparse because of the many large and trivial differences in assumptions, expectations, experiences and symbol structures between Indian and non-Indian. The American Indian writer has difficulty locating readers/listeners who can comprehend the significance of her work, even when she is being as clear and direct as she can be, because these differences in experience and meaning assigned to events create an almost impossible barrier (*Sacred Hoop* 156-7).

Overcoming this "almost impossible barrier" was an important goal of Allen's lifework. As a teacher, she was what Gloria Anzaldua called a *nepantlera*, a psycho-spiritual bridge-builder whose role is to act as a channel of communication across differ-ence in the service of solidarity. "Though tempted to retreat behind racial lines and hide behind simplistic walls of identity, *las nepantleras* know their work lies in positioning themselves—exposed and raw—in the crack between these worlds, and in revealing current categories as unworkable," says Anzaldua ("Now Let Us Shift" 567). Allen herself described her scholarly practice as "somewhat western and somewhat Indian. I draw from each, and in the end I often wind up with a reasonably accurate picture of the truth" (*Sacred Hoop* 7). In keeping with her role as a *nepantlera*, Allen's publications are all aimed at educating general American audiences—Native and non-Native alike—about Native American culture, particularly the women's traditions that she saw as having been neglected by earlier scholars.

> Women's rituals, ceremonies, traditions, customs, attitudes, values, activities, philosophies, ceremonial and social posi-tions, histories, medicine societies and shamanistic identi-ties—that is, all the oral tradition that is in every sense and on every level the literature of the tribes—have been largely ignored by folklorists, ethnographers and literary critics in the field of American Indian studies. These traditions have never been described or examined in terms of their proper, that is, woman-focused, context. Actually, it is primarily the context that has been ignored—vanished, disappeared, bur-ied under tons of scholarly materials selected and erected to hide the centrality of women in tribal society, tribal litera-ture and tribal hearts and minds . . . (*Sacred Hoop* 268).

Allen recognized that women's contributions to the oral and writ-ten literature of the tribes formed a key context without which understandings of tribal cultures would be skewed in the direction of the male traditions. Yet it wasn't simply a matter of reversing the poles and foregrounding women's actions and roles; it was a question of creating balance by learning to see through Native eyes.

> It is the nature of woman's existence to be and to create background. This fact, viewed with unhappiness by many feminists, is of ultimate importance in a tribal context . . . Westerners have for a long time discounted the importance of background. The earth herself, which is our most inclusive background, is dealt with summarily as a source of food, metals, water and profit, while the fact that she is the fundamental agent of all planetary life is blithely ignored. Similarly, women's activities . . . are devalued . . . In the western mind, shadows highlight the foreground. In contrast, in the tribal view the mutual relationships among shadows and light . . . create a living web of definition and depth, and significance arises from their interplay (*Sacred Hoop* 243-44).

The last paragraph of *The Sacred Hoop* returns to this central insight. "By the simple expedient of shifting the view back to its original and rightful position," Allen says, with female and male traditions balanced, "the whole picture changes, and it becomes clear that our heart is in the sky. We understand that woman is the sun and the earth; she is grandmother; she is mother; she is Thought, Wisdom, Dream, Reason, Tradition, Memory, Deity and Life itself. Nos Vemos" (*Sacred Hoop* 268).

Unlike Gloria Anzaldua, Allen rarely uses Spanish in her writing, and yet we find that phrase, "*Nos Vemos*," as the last words in two of her most important books, *The Sacred Hoop* (quoted above) and *Grandmothers of the Light*. She ends *Grandmothers of the Light* on a note of prophecy:

> Based on their sacred calendar, Maya prophecies testify that

quite soon this world will take a turn in its long spiral path around the center of the galaxy returning us to our more usual place (or psychic space) in the cosmos. By the mid twenty-first century we will be more and more aware of the presence of the supernaturals among us. I hope that this volume will aid in the process of return, enabling women to recover our ancient medicine ways and once again establish our ongoing relation to the Great Mystery. Nos vemos. (*Grandmothers* 233).

In Spanish, the phrase "*nos vemos*" is usually tossed off in a casual manner, as in the English "See you later." Literally it means "we'll see each other," or possibly, "we'll see ourselves." Allen may have had all of these meanings in mind in choosing to end two of her books on this note, but given the all-important context into which the Spanish words are set, they take on a deeper significance: In that time, in that place, in the practice of that tradition, we women will see each other, and ourselves, more clearly, as we really are. Significantly, and typically, Allen does not exclude non-Native women from participating in the re-establishment of "our on-going relation to the Great Mystery." Although she doesn't mention men, she stresses throughout her work that men's traditions are equal and complementary to women's — just not her focus, given her position as a woman.

Allen writes as a "citizen of two worlds" (*Grandmothers* 21): melding past and present, ordinary and non-ordinary reality, male and female characters into stories that affirm again and again the enduring flame of the human spirit, which, she says, burns most brightly through the feminine traditions. Working within the academic field of literary studies, she conceives her field broadly enough to include anthropology and folklore. She seeks to have an impact not just on these scholarly fields, but more ambitiously on the future of human life on the planet itself, which she sees as deeply linked to human spiritual interaction with the non-physical realms. Allen's planetary vision sees our time as "the time referred to in ancient prophecy: the time when the clans come in and the blue star Kachina dances in the village square, when the Grandmother goddesses return and Native Americans lead the world into a new age of peace, balance, harmony and respect for all that is (*Grandmothers* x).

Allen doesn't waste time with bitter retrospective rehashings of the traumatic history of Native America since the arrival of Europeans. Instead she works to save the knowledge that has survived, in the hopes of leading humanity and the entire interconnected planet into a better time, a sixth sun. This new age will be born not of strife and fire, but of patient attention and the passing of knowledge from one generation to the next. In the final story of *Grandmothers of the Light*, "Someday Soon," Allen even goes so far as to suggest that it will be Native and non-Native peoples working together who will see the world safely into the new, wiser age.

"Someday Soon" is Allen's mythical retelling of a story that some have dismissed as apocryphal: the story of the discovery of a quartz crystal skull in the ruins of the lost Mayan city of Lubaatún in Belize, by the adventurer F.A. Mitchell-Hedges. All of the details of this story have been debated over the years by journalists and other investigators. Was the flamboyant Mitchell-Hedges really accompanied at the ruins by his adopted daughter, Anna? Did he really leave little Anna with the local Mayans for seven years? Did she really find the crystal skull flashing through a hole in the ruin, or was it planted there by her adopted father as a birthday present/prank? Anna Mitchell-Hedges, who lived to be 100 years old and passed away in 2007, spent much of her own adventurous life furthering the mystique of the skull, which she claimed was a pre-Columbian Mayan sacred artifact. Experts disagree on whether the Mitchell-Hedges crystal skull, like other similar relics housed in museums and private collections throughout the world, are really ancient Mayan sacred totems, or are actually sophisticated fakes, made in the 19th century. Allen does not engage with these controversies, although in her introduction to "Someday Soon" she does mention having traveled to Canada herself to visit Anna Mitchell-Hedges (not mentioned by name) and see the famous skull for herself:

> The Crystal Skull, the amazing crystallized remains of the immortal I have called Crystal Woman, was found in Mopán country early this century. Studied by archaeologists, visited by seekers, and filmed by the men who quested among the Maya and discovered the Skull in the process, this being (I can't call her an artifact!) is a powerful and beautiful presence. I was honored to have channeled information from her when I visited her home in Canada in the summer of 1987. Much of what she told me is included in this story (*Grandmothers* 195).

Allen's story "Someday Soon" shifts the account of the crystal skull into a mythic register, with Allen describing in the lyrical, repetitive cadences of traditional Indigenous storytelling how the thirteen ancient immortals she calls "the Women of Wisdom" came to reside in the caves in "Mopán country" (present-day Belize, not named as such in the story). She alludes to the popular belief that these ancient wise women came from Atlantis: "the waters returned in a rush, and the lands they had left were drowned" (*Grandmothers* 196). As ancient immortals, they

> *infused their cells, all their flesh and bone, with the knowing.*
> *In that time . . . they danced and chanted, chanted and*
> *danced . . . In those long years, they perfected their skills and*

*made into flesh every word they said. And then at last it was fin-
ished, all but the sacrifice was done. They lay still and deep within
their bodies, quiet and at rest within their sacred flesh ... And as
they lay there their flesh became stone ... They slowly over this
time abstracted their being, their consciousness, from their flesh.
They entered another kind of being that mortals call air, fire,
spirit (Grandmothers 197).*

Allen continues, telling of the discovery of these crystallized
remains by the Mayan "priestesses and shamans" who, venturing
deep into the cavernous chambers of the earth, "found the thirteen
bodies made of stone laid out perfectly, their limbs ordered in alignment, their heads to the west" (*Grandmothers* 198). The shamans
take the head of one of these crystal bodies and bring it to their own
stone citadel, where "for generations, they used ... [it] to gain
knowledge and to see to the needs of the people," until gradually, in
time, the people "fell into conflict" and the "temples fell and were
buried beneath the proliferation of green" (*Grandmothers* 199). The
crystal skull lay forgotten in the ruins, until one day, the "maiden"
Allen calls "Dawn Light Girl," walking over the partially excavated
ruins, "looked down" and "saw a small but unmistakable flash of
light" (*Grandmothers* 200). Here Allen relies on the version of the
story told by Anna Mitchell-Hedges, who described finding the
skull as she clambered over the ruins of Lubaatún on her 17th birthday. The debate over whether or not Anna's story was "true" clearly
does not interest Allen, who is after the deeper meanings that can
be read into sacred objects like the crystal skull. Her lack of concern
over the superficial veracity of the story is illustrated by her choice
to expose multiple facets of possibility as she continues her account:

*It is said the Indians were joyful. They danced and sang for days.
They erected a brush shelter and for miles around they came to
pay homage. 'Our Grandmother is restored to us,' they said.*

> *It is said they were unhappy, stricken that their crystal was thus exposed, that they came for days to bid her good-bye.*
>
> *In time the headman from far away left the region. He took his daughter and the skull away. It is said the people tried to keep it, but the white man refused. 'I must take it for safekeeping,' he told them.*
>
> *It is also said the headman said to the people, 'I cannot take this with me. You must keep it because it is yours.' But the people demurred, saying, 'No. It was found by your daughter, Sun Woman. It must stay with her.' And so saying, they parted, the man, his daughter and the immortal woman's bones went north, went east. The people, the forests and the fallen temples stayed (Grandmothers 200).*

In Allen's re-telling, this is not a story about the theft of sacred Mayan artifacts by white explorers; she is not interested in determining the "scientific" origin of the crystal skull, or in lamenting the fact that it is now owned by a North American and housed far away from the Mayan people. Rather, it is a story about the possibility of cooperation and respect between different peoples, over many generations, in the interests of planetary harmony. The last part of the story focuses on "two American men," one "Native American . . . the other a spiritual seeker of Middle Eastern Christian descent" who went to Belize to make a film about the ancient Mayans (*Grandmothers* 195). "As was proper," Allen says, "the two men brought gifts and food to the south on their journeys, taking care of the people as the people took care of them" (*Grandmothers* 201). Following the trail of the crystal skull, they also "made their way far to the north, to the crisp suburban home of Sun Woman, Daughter of Light," where "as was proper, the two men paid their respects to Old Sun Woman and her companion, and aided them as they could (*Grandmothers* 201). Out of this respectful exchange, Allen foresees and foretells the coming of a new age, a new beginning, when "the Goddess will return in the fullness of her being. It is said that the Mother of All and Everything, the Grandmother of the Sun and the Dawn, will return to her children and with her will come harmony, peace and the healing of the world. It is said that time is coming. Soon" (*Grandmothers* 201).

As is typical of her work, Allen uses myth to promote social and spiritual healing; her stories are guideposts on the path to a wiser, more harmonious age, an age she foretold but did not live to see. Like the crystal skull, which Allen imagined as a repository of supernatural wisdom and a link between the spiritual and material planes of existence, her writings also function as ritual paeans to sacred stories, to ancient Indigenous wisdom in danger of being lost to humanity. Writing becomes a ritual for her, a way to honor the ancestors and educate her contemporaries, while preparing the way for a more positive future the earth and its inhabitants.

We live today on the razor's edge between survival and annihilation: we are as close to destroying ourselves, and a great deal of life on the planet with us, as we have ever come, thanks to our over-reliance on technology and our lack of attention to the all-important context, our Mother Earth. Allen, who would ultimately herself fall victim to asthma, emphysema and lung cancer, believed that

> *disease is a symptom of spiritual disorder, but whether that disorder is the fault of the sufferers is another matter entirely. Indeed, there are powerful arguments advanced in Indian country that many of us suffer from a variety of immune system disorders and other chronic debilitations because we are earth's children, and as she endures monstrous patriarchal abuse, we suffer as well, sharing in her pain and disease and in that way ameliorating its devastation and bringing some respite to her (Grandmothers 169).*

Intentionally or not, it is clear that human beings and other living beings on this planet are sharing in the disorders we have wreaked on our environment—as we have poisoned our air, water and earth, we have also poisoned ourselves, with diseases like asthma and cancer the obvious physical manifestations of the imbalance. Writing in 1991, Allen drew attention to a phenomenon of extinction that has only accelerated in the intervening years:

> Right now, countless numbers of animal and plant species are following Grandmother's trail. They are leaving us to our own devices, rendering the planet more and more bleak and empty. Traditionals say that so long as modern people continue in their depredations of the planet, spewing negative thinking, disharmony and disrespect for all that lives, famine, drought, and the loss of vast numbers of life forms will continue to accelerate. Even the air is leaving. Violating taboos is very dangerous to all life, and while most Americans can blithely avoid the immediate consequences of disrespect, the human community over most of the world pays a very high price indeed for our violations. (*Grandmothers* 170)

In the age of global climate change, Americans can no longer afford to "blithely" ignore or avoid the consequences of our disrespectful approach to Mother Earth, and there are some good signs that we have begun to heed the wisdom offered us by the Native traditions (although often without giving due credit to the source of our 'new,' more balanced philosophy).

Allen, seeing life as a great spiral dance rather than a linear progression from birth to death, always focused on the upswing, the return, the continuity of existence: "There is surely reason to weep, to grieve; but greater than ugliness, the endurance of tribal beauty is our reason to sing, to greet the coming day and the restored hope and life it brings" (*Grandmothers* xi). Following her model, this is what we too should focus on, as the days tick off one by one towards the future. There are those who predict that Armageddon—chaos and destruction—will be our lot in the rapidly approaching year 2012. Allen, following Native tradition, thought otherwise: "The Mopán Maya of Belize say that the new age will begin in 2012, when an era of harmony, peace and renewal will be ushered in" (*Grandmothers* 195). If her prediction is right, it will be in no small part due to her own hard work in preserving and furthering the wisdom of Native women's spiritual traditions.

To end with the prayer she taught us: "May the Grandmothers of the Light bring us dawn. May we welcome and aid them in the growing light" (*Grandmothers* xiv).

The Place & Places of Paula Gunn Allen

Joseph Bruchac III

I'm holding in my hand a copy of an anthology I edited 33 years ago: *Songs From This Earth On Turtle's Back, Contemporary American Indian Poetry.* Fifty-two writers were included in what some called a ground-breaking book back then, many of whom are now regarded as among the most significant Native writers of the 20th century—such authors as Linda Hogan, Maurice Kenny, N. Scott Momaday, Simon J. Ortiz, Leslie Silko, Gerald Vizenor, James Welch, Ray A. Young Bear.

But it is especially meaningful to me that the first writer in that admittedly alphabetically arranged collection was none other than Paula Gunn Allen.

It seems to me, as I scan the recent critical literature, that Paula's place as an important voice, a seminal voice, and one that is both unique and powerful, has not been fully acknowledged. And not merely as a Native American poet and essayist, but as one who spoke to our generation of writers in general, who never avoided controversy, who was unafraid to put herself on the cutting edge, and whose work always acknowledged her debt to the ancestors and the earth. Although it hasn't quite happened yet, I believe that her importance, her reputation and readership will continue to grow.

The books, essays, and anthologies that Paula published in the years following that 1983 volume are a testament to her energy, her wide-ranging mind and her spirit. Others have addressed that later work of hers, her unavoidable presence as a prolific poet, a perceptive literary critic, and lesbian activist in the quarter century that followed. But what I would like to focus on is a bit of what Paula wrote back then—by way of an introduction to herself and her poetics.

When I put together *Songs From This Earth on Turtle's Back*, I decided to do two things in addition to including the widest possible range of American Indian poets. I asked each writer to choose which work of theirs would be included. That way more than my own personal taste would be reflected. I also asked each poet to write her or his own bio note. Some of the resulting notes were short, but not Paula's. She produced two full pages that remain as eloquent a statement of politics, poetics and personality as anything I have ever read. I recommend that "bio note" to anyone interested not just in Paula, or in Native poetry, but in the truth of Language.

As proof of that, here are two passages from it. This first is a picture of Paula as she saw herself, a word portrait flavored by the slightly self-deprecating humor that characterized so much of what Paula wrote—without ever diminishing the brilliance of what she was and what she had to say.

> *"When you're a halfbreed, a daughter of both Laguna and Lebanon; when you're raised in Cubero where almost everyone speaks Spanish, New Mexico style; when your granddaddy is Jewish from Germany—not Orthodox, not Reformed, just born of Jews; when your whole family's lives are obscure in America, revised, disappeared; when you think Main Street is a small*

dusty road that winds its way Uptown—to the rest of the small village you call home; when only one of the five languages your family converses in is English—you're bound to be a bit challenging to understand. And when your mother is a daughter of the last gynocracy on earth, and your father a son of an ancient patriarchy, you're bound to write difficult poetry; you're bound to be a bit of an oddity in America, or anywhere at all."

This second quote is as pure a rebuttal as I've ever read of a certain attitude about poetry that so often came into play in the late 20th century as, to be frank, a way of dismissing most poets, black, yellow, red, gay, lesbian, or just plain political, whose work was meant to speak truth to power.

"McLeish opined that 'a poem should not mean but be,' and Jan Clausen said that poetics of use is not possible and is a dangerous notion. But where I come from beautiful and useful are synonymous, and useful is always beauty full, always meaningful, given the context, given that one knows who is the mother of the item under consideration. I think a world that does not want meaning is a very strange world for a human being to operate in . . . I cannot imagine a meal that is not of use, and thus beautiful; I cannot imagine wanting such a meal that is without meaning."

That is so Paula. Whenever I read it, I can see the look on her face, that smile of hers that you can see in the photo of her in the book, a photo taken while she was visiting us in Greenfield Center in 1982—along with her then "poet girlfriend" as Paula put it, Judy Grahn (who, like Paula, was born in New Mexico). As I recall, I took that picture as Paula was talking about the fact that she had recently found her first gray hair on her head—an occasion which led her to have a party for all her women friends to celebrate that gray hair, the first visible sign that she was entering into the much to be desired stage of her life of being an elder.

A year or two later, when I was visiting Albuquerque, I spent a more than memorable day with Paula. It began with her directing my attention to the mountain that can be seen from just about everywhere in the town, a mountain whose shape is like that of a great turtle, a mountain that she said truly marked her place in the world.

"I always miss it when I'm away," Paula said. "If you listen close, you can hear it breathing."

And then, switching gears, she asked me what I considered a curious question. "Would you like to see some old Indian ruins?" "Okay," I said, even though the usual tourist things do not generally interest me. But, knowing Paula, I figured she had something interesting in store. Then, instead of taking me out of town, she drove me to a high-rise building, hit the button for the top floor, led me to an apartment where her knock on the door was answered by her mother and her grandmother. "Let me introduce you," she said, "to two old Indian ruins." Indian humor par excallance.

And, once again, it was pure Paula, that combination of trickster and mystic that she pulled off so well because, quite frankly, that is who she was. As well as a poet who did not hesitate to turn that little prank she pulled on me into her poem "Taking a Visitor to See the Ruins."

It is still difficult for me to believe that it has been eight years since her passing in 2008. Paula was, no is, one of those people whose presence always went beyond the merely physical. I know that for her family and friends—who loved her dearly—the fact that the words of "a little half-breed girl" (as she sometimes called herself) have gone far beyond her beloved mountains and mesas is no substitute for her physical presence. But for those touched by her words—and those still to be informed and inspired by them in the future—Paula's place will long be secure in our minds and in our hearts.

Mestiza Nation

A Future History of My Tribe

Deborah Miranda

The original acts of colonization and violence broke the world, broke our hearts, broke the connection between soul and flesh. For many of us, this trauma happens again in each generation, as children too young and too untrained try to cope with dysfunction that ravages even adults. Gloria Anzaldua knew this. Paula Gunn Allen knew this. Chicana, Indian, these women knew that the formation of a Mestiza Nation was as much about healing from our childhoods as healing from larger histories.

I am of the seventh generation since my great-great-great-great-great-great grandparents, Fructuoso Cholom and Yginina Yunisyunis, emerged from Mission San Carlos de Borromeo in Carmel, California in the mid-1830's. I am half white, half Indian, mixed with Mexican and Jewish tribes. When I look at all that has passed since Fructuoso Cholom and Yginia Yunisyunis were emancipated, I wonder if they dreamed that their descendants would still be struggling to free ourselves, seven generations later.

When I look toward the next seven generations, I imagine this is the kind of story that my descendants will tell, seven generations from now, in the future mythology of the Mestiza Nation.

Once there was a girl without a mother.

She'd never had a mother, even though she called the woman who gave birth to her *Mama*. This woman kept leaving her daughter behind at relative's homes or forgetting her in stores. It wasn't entirely Mama's fault; often when she thought her arms were full of little girl, or that the little girl was safely clutching Mama's hand, it was really the ghost of a daughter Mama had lost years ago.

So when Mama felt the weight of a child heavy against her hip or tugging at her arm, she didn't know it was actually the pull of persistent sorrow distracting her from the real child. Sometimes the real little girl caught sight of her dead sister, hungrily wrapping her chubby arms around Mama's neck as they went out the door together, leaving the little girl once again. Sometimes the little girl's father followed them.

Her father was why the little girl was different from her older sister and brother. They were light-skinned, with clear blue eyes and hair the color of cornflakes. But the girl without a mother was cinnamon-colored, with thick dark hair, vivid against her family. When the girl without a mother held hands with her brother or sister to cross the street, their long slender fingers seem to tangle up with her wide flat palms and short fingers. At the park, no one listened to the little girl when she claimed her brother and sister, not even when the big sister yelled at the bullies trying to push her off the swing.

The girl without a mother began to understand that she was invisible. She wondered if this was why her Ghost Sister had become a ghost in the first place; if she herself were becoming less and less real, too.

Eventually the woman who gave birth to the little girl went away and didn't come back. Secretly, the girl thought perhaps her mother was looking for the girl's father, who had been missing for some time now. The big sister didn't tell anyone, but bathed her little brother and sister each night, fed them cereal each morning, sent the boy off to school, dropped the little girl off at a babysitter's. The big sister brushed the little girl's hair, and helped the little brother with his homework, but one day, the food ran out, and the big sister had to call a grown-up. The older brother and sister were taken to a foster home, a place for children without parents. But the home only had space for older children. *Bring the little one back in the fall,* said the people in charge. *We might have room then.*

That is how the girl without a mother came to stay with her mother's parents for one short season.

※

Her mother's parents were light-skinned and blue-eyed as well, but in those days it was common for such people to settle in the very land from which the little girl's father and his people had emerged. The girl loved her grandmother's house in the dry Tehachapi Mountains; she spent the summer playing with lizards and horned toads, sleeping between cool cotton sheets, watching the glimmer of hummingbirds come to her grandmother's feeder very early in the morning. Her dark eyes feasted on the sagebrush dotting the brown hills, and she spoke regularly with a black bird perched in the manzanita behind the house. She ran barefoot all day, her feet finding joy in the dust. Once, she sat down on some ants who were busy with their own matters, and was badly bitten. Later, after apologizing to the ants, the little girl watched them work for hours, at a distance.

Every evening the grandmother bathed the girl in a deep shiny white tub, but no matter how the woman scrubbed, the colors wrought by soil and sun would not be cleansed from the girl's knees and cheeks.

"More like that man every day," the grandfather muttered to himself, shaking his head. "The sooner they have room for her at Mrs. Samm's the better."

But the grandmother saw her own lost daughter in this little girl's movements, and wished for a chance to correct her mistakes as a mother. The grandmother let the girl without a mother sow corn in the small fenced flower garden, where the green stalks were watered generously each evening along with the morning glories, petunias, pansies, tall daisies and brilliant orange poppies.

When the corn reached the girl's waist, the foster family called: they still had no room for the girl without a mother. The grandfather silenced the grandmother's look with a curt "no." The grandmother turned away.

No one asked the girl where she would like to live. She would have chosen to stay and see the corn grow past her head. But one day before the sun was up, her grandmother came to wake her for a trip to a yet another place.

~\|/~

The girl without a mother stood on the steps of her grandmother's house. Behind her rose a mountain, dark and seemingly still. Before her rose the sky, arched black and brilliant with stars, and the cleft of a long valley. The air was dry, cool, gently opening.

From her grandmother's garden came the smooth slippery surge of petunias, snapdragons, poppies. The happy leaves of the corn plants shivered with pleasure as they grew upwards in their slow spiral. The girl without a mother stood alone, huddled in a soft sweater, wearing only a sundress underneath because it would be hot later. Inside the house, her grandmother packed sandwiches and thermoses of coffee and milk. The grandmother cried as she tightened the lids of containers.

No person saw this; only the grandmother's heart knew this grief that she would not speak of until she was a very old woman, many thousands of miles away from this place, dying, and asking for-giveness. In the garage, the grandfather loaded up the truck that would take the girl without a mother away. He would start the motor any minute.

But for one moment before dawn the world was humming with quiet power, and the girl without a mother heard a funny sound.

Thump and pause. *Thump* and pause. Scraps of a song wandered in between the sounds. It almost seemed to be asking a question, a question the girl couldn't quite hear all the words to, but that she wanted to answer. *Thump,* pause. *Thump,* pause, *song.*

The girl went quickly down the wooden steps and around the back of the house, stepping carefully around the gopher traps she'd watched her grandfather set. *Thump,* pause. *Song, song, song.* The girl wandered into a dry streambed, followed the stones. The rocks were washed and smooth and she could see where to put her feet better and more easily the longer she climbed; the sun was follow-ing behind her.

She climbed and climbed. When the girl without a mother got

tired, a woman came to meet her, and took her through the side of the mountain. *Come here, this way,* the woman said; she picked up her grinding stone and basket, pushed aside a curtain of dried grasses and sticks. *We are little rabbits looking for our nest,* she smiled, *we are fawns, called to our mother's side in the warm grass.* And the girl without a mother followed the song of the woman who came out of a mountain.

Inside the opening was a cool, sandy tunnel. The darkness seemed soft, like a light blanket, not frightening at all. After only a few steps, the two came out into another place, a land with a stream full of big silver fish swimming lazily in from the sea, seemingly straight into the nets and hands of laughing men; oak trees covered thick green hills. Under the heavy branches, families with baskets gathered acorns, children played while they worked, women were easy with their voices. The girl without a mother noticed right away that some of the people were darker than her, and some of them were lighter.

The woman who came out of a mountain gestured to the new place. *See, this is where you will live now.*

Are you going to be my mother? asked the girl without a mother, taking off her blue sweater and letting it slide to the ground.

No, I'm just an old woman, laughed the woman who came out of a mountain. *Not many children here have mothers. But you'll be cared for. This is getting to be a big family. We're busy just now—acorns, salmon, islay are good this year. You'll have to help.*

By now the little girl had stripped off her sundress, and her black patent leather shoes that squished her toes, and the white slippery socks that made her feet sweat. She stood in itchy underwear that got caught in all the wrong places but had been her secret armor against the dark. Hardly anyone here wore clothes except for pretty, she noticed; but most girls her age had a rustley skirt. *Can I have one of those?* she asked, pointing to two girls running by with empty baskets in their arms. *And a basket like that for working?*

The woman who came out of a mountain reached out and stopped the other children. *This is the girl I went to find,* explained the woman. *Help her make a skirt, and give her a basket. She'll work with you.*

The three girls looked at each other. The girl without a mother was astonished. One of the girls had a dark, serious face much like her own—short nose, arched eyebrows, thin lips—but freckles washed across her cheeks. Her eyes sparkled black and made the girl rise on her tiptoes with a laugh. Her hair was shiny black and thick, like the little girl's, too.

The second girl stood light and alive, as if she could hardly keep from dancing away; her skin was the color of sand in the river, and her eyes glimmered brown and green like water over deep rocks. Yet her hair had the same still darkness as her companion's.

The girl without a mother knew with a certainty that here were others who had not matched their families.

Suddenly both girls smiled, and the girl without a mother, who had no brothers or sisters who looked the way she did, felt a grin blossom on her own face. Some scar sealed shut in her chest opened; warm, strong, blood rushed in.

The first girl held out a round basket, revealing her wide flat palm and short strong fingers.

You can have this one, she said.

It was all a long time ago, longer than anyone remembers. On the other side of the tunnel, people searched for the girl without a mother. They had dogs who tracked her faint scent up a rocky streambed, farther than anyone believed she could have walked. But even the dogs couldn't find any sign past a place where the arroyo curved sharply around a big hill dense with sagebrush and rabbit holes.

Long after the little girl's corn had ripened, taller than the grandmother and heavy with fat ears, the grandparents ceased looking. The foster family didn't have room for the many other children in that place without mothers, anyway. People slowly forgot about the girl without a mother, though her grandmother came out before dawn and listened hard for music she was almost afraid to hear.

Every once in awhile the woman who came out of a mountain went back, pushed aside the curtain of sagebrush and manzanita, and looked out. She could see a long, long way from her hill; clearly, too.

Sometimes her sharp eyes caught sight of a certain kind of child. Then the woman who came out of a mountain would take her grinding stones and basket, sit by the entrance, and sing. If the child were very small, the woman would walk quietly down the streambed to meet him. If the child were older, the woman sang soothing songs to encourage her.

None of the children who came to her ever arrived unharmed, but the woman who came out of a mountain always took them home with her anyway.

This is the song she sang:

Ah hey way lo lo, hey way
lo lo, hey way lo-lo;
Lo lo, hey-hey, ah hey way
lo lo, hey way lo-lo;
A hey way lo lo, hey way
lo lo, hey way lo-lo
lo lo hey hey
hey way lo lo
hey way lo lo
lo lo hey hey
ah hey way lo lo
hey way lo lo
hey way lo lo . . .

WE CONTINUE TO WEAVE

El Morro
Kristina Bitsue

Writing the Good Fight

Stephanie A. Sellers

During my first conversation with Paula Gunn Allen, when I asked her to advise my doctoral work in Native American Studies, she told me plainly, "*I don't want to fight anymore.*"

She was referring to the non-Native members of my doctoral committee and her desire to not enter another situation where she would have to exert effort arguing, explaining, and legitimizing Indigenous history, experience, and literature to the most likely misguided and misinformed faculty.

She said, "*I'm tired.*"

I assured her that I did not believe there would be any arguing involved about the basics. At the time I already did understand what she was talking about in terms of Native struggles with academia; however, now twelve years after graduation with a doctorate in Native American Studies (NAS), I can look back and say that I did not have any idea about the magnitude of what was coming at me full force. Paula had already been fighting the ignorance and prejudices in academia for decades before we met, and I witnessed the effects of those struggles on her health. But after earning my Ph.D., I quickly learned they would become my struggles as well.

Here is a memorable example: Many years ago I was contacted by a former student who had been enrolled in several of my Native American Studies courses. She is a EuroAmerican graduate student who, at the time, had a full scholarship to study colonial-era history at a prestigious university in the American northeast. When we spoke on the telephone she was disillusioned and shocked. She relayed to me that her graduate advisor, a well-known American history scholar, refers to only EuroAmerican settlers as "Native Americans" and Native peoples as "Indians" in all his lectures. She said that her graduate courses in American colonial history include no texts by Native scholars and largely implicate Native "lack of cooperation" as the cause of Native wars with the colonizers. With anger and confusion in her voice, my former student kept saying to me, "How could this be? How do they get away with this?"

I told her, *"You have entered the fight."*

Over my two decades of teaching so far, this same story would be repeated to me by former students over and over again. Though the graduate school institutions changed and their experiences began to include national and state historical sites and public school systems where they had gained employment, the story from their mentors and supervisors remained the same: Indians were problems to the peaceful settlers and today "culturally-authentic" Indians are as extinct as the brontosaurus. The wall of ignorance coming at Native American Studies scholars and our students is as hulking and menacing as those first tall ships landing at Plymouth Rock. As a NAS scholar and a woman of Cherokee heritage, I learned that my struggles were going to be magnified in ways that my EuroAmerican male NAS colleagues do not experience.

Paula often said to me, "It's not going to be easy, you know, working in academia. There are other ways to make a living. Are you sure you want to do this?"

My teaching experience in NAS has certainly encompassed unexpected extremes: from outright hatred and sadistic marginalization to admiration, respect, and radical inclusion. Institutions of higher learning in America are primary sites where colonial battles are still being waged and fought; and who supports NAS or fights against it can be surprising and disappointing. I will start by sharing the difficult lessons and finish my essay with the joy and rewards.

I thought I understood what I was getting into when I took my first job as a professor, but in hindsight, I was utterly naïve and foolishly believed that simply teaching cultural and historical information can eradicate ignorance around Native American cultures and histories. For most people learning does change them; but for many others, you can point forever at the wampum and birch bark books and they are still going to argue that Indigenous Eastern Woodlanders were (and still are) illiterate. Ethnocentrism is powerful and blinding; it defies intellectual processes even when the person has a Ph.D. because that person is functioning within a system of hierarchy. That's what I had to learn.

Teaching NAS is not just about transmission of Indigenous histories and cultures; it is about challenging a core component of identity that many Americans do not realize they have founded their existence upon. Many Americans would be surprised to see within themselves how profoundly their own sense of self is tied up with their belief in the sanctity of George Washington, for example. When I point out that he is referred to as the Town Destroyer or He Burns It by Eastern Woodlanders, people can get very defensive, very angry. This is what NAS scholars are up against. Doing this work asks many people in the academy to look at something in themselves and in their country that they do not want to see. My pedagogical approaches have changed quite a bit over the years, and I can see the results in the positive learning responses in my students. Helping them with the struggle incurred by the learning is imperative if a lasting impact is going to be made that will change how America thinks about Indigenous history and Indigenous nations today. I have to be a facilitator of their journey, not just their teacher.

Issues of legitimacy and authority play key roles in assessing scholarly materials and are also part of the colonial challenges at work for NAS scholars. This was a first battle I had to face as a professor. Today, a EuroAmerican "expert" (anyone with a Ph.D.) still has far greater power in the legal system over the testimony of an Indigenous person, even trumping the testimonies of recognized tribal leaders. This has powerful ramifications over Indigenous sovereignty and land rights. Over the course of centuries, women-generated sources (diaries, letters, memoir) and sources from people of color were considered academically unreliable, and their testimonies were often inadmissible, or at least suspect, in courts of law—and still are. Hence, the power to claim what is admissible and legitimate academically and legally has always been in the hands of those with privilege and power, and assessment of academic sources has simply never existed purely as a truth-seeking endeavor that brings a complete human narrative into scholarly discourse. The process of determining academic and legal legitimacy stands out starkly clear in Native American Studies where some (highly influential) non-Indigenous peoples still deride the Keepings/oral traditions and wampum records, and deeply suspect and attempt to discredit Indigenous Keepers, traditionals, and NAS scholars in general. Doing so is not a scholarly process, but is about the power to determine whose voice matters and whose does not: a colonial process to the core.

Knowledge can also be confiscated and "owned" by an imperialist entity that determines the histories and experiences of the colonized by controlling and disseminating a narrative about them. Acts of domination, colonization, and empire are still committed in relation to Indigenous people's knowledge, histories, and cultures. There is no such thing as post-colonial—I always ask colleagues who claim otherwise, *"When did colonization end?"* Land, natural resources like water, gold and oil, and culture are not the only things that can be colonized. I only wish the colonization of Indigenous knowledge no longer occurred in newly published scholarship, which makes my job so much more difficult. There are many examples, but I will provide only the following from highly-visible and lauded scholars: 1) A nationally-recognized colonial-era history scholar dismissively states in a PBS documentary, *We Shall Remain*, that Native Americans were simply "caught in history"; 2) A colonial-era historian who won an American Book Award and was a nominee for the Pulitzer Prize writes in a 2006 volume that Sir William Johnson's access to the Iroquois people was through his "mistress" Molly Brant whom Johnson "bedded" to gain diplomatic access to her people. [Tekonwatonti (Molly Brant) was a Mohawk Clan Mother and a major military leader in the 1700s—her *status in her nation* provided the diplomatic privileges her husband Johnson enjoyed, as those privileges run in the women's lineages/purview.]; 3) Last, a 2017 winner of an American Book Award, and a brilliant researcher on American race issues, stated on a May 25, 2017 National Public Radio interview on the program "1A" that race issues in America began with African slavery. Such a distinguished researcher making this outrageous statement that ignores Indigenous existence speaks to the depth of the problem America has in relation to its history.

The colonial narrative continues to thrive in academia, as professors build lucrative careers by promulgating it with impunity. It does not help that we NAS scholars are still drastically outnumbered in higher education and have to shout above the din of credentialed colonial voices.

Some highlights of my troubling, even traumatic, experiences at several institutions where I have been a professor over the past twenty years include receiving an email from an English department chair telling me I could forget ever having full-time employment in the English department of that public university because "the writing of Native Americans is not American literature." I was told pointedly during a job interview by a Dean of the College of Arts and Humanities at the third-ranking liberal arts college in the country that, "There are only a handful of real Native Americans left and they all live on a reservation—and they're originally from Africa anyway though they deny it!" Another experience: the chair of a Diversity and Inclusion committee at a very small public institution where I had been employed for over a decade asked me when we met, "So what do you teach here, Stephanie?" When I organized a student panel from my Native American Studies course at a Big Ten school, I was told by a vice provost that "if you think this is going to get you somewhere down the road, it's not!" A last highlight, and one of the most memorable, is when a colleague erupted in uncontrollable laughter when I was introduced to him on campus as the university's only instructor in Native American literatures. When he finally regained the ability to speak, he blurted, "How can you teach Native American literature when Indians can't write?!" The faculty who introduced me to him stood in mute shock, embarrassed and apologetic only when we were alone. What can only out-best this one is when another vice-provost at a different institution asked me if I had a campus mailbox—I had been working there for eight years! When I stared blankly at her, she helped me with my confusion by adding "it would be in your home department." Thank you. Thank you so much for clarifying.

The most ludicrous experience I had, which I can only laugh about now, occurred at my first job as a contingency faculty member over twenty years ago. After a few months on campus at this school teaching Native American writers in my English courses, I was invited to speak at the monthly lecture for the faculty. I felt honored. I immediately thought "maybe I'm not going to have it as badly as my traditional Native teachers had it —maybe things have changed somewhat in my generation." Five minutes into my talk, the host professor interrupted me with a question—he seemed irritated. About 20-minutes later he was red-faced, attacking me, even raising his voice about topics I was not even addressing. He said angrily, "Anyone can have a sweatlodge!" and "Movies do not have to convey authentic Native culture because they are for entertainment!" The tenured faculty in the room said nothing, though they appeared to be visibly disturbed. I realized later that my invitation had been a total set-up! This host professor was intent on demonstrating to me that he was the authority in NAS on campus, not me. I now refer to this type of behavior as "Unresolved Boy Scout Syndrome"—little did I realize then that I would be seeing a lot more of this behavior in years to come. Over the next year before I left this school, whenever I ran into this man he would glare at me, walk on a different sidewalk when he saw me, and shake his head and mutter angrily under his breath around me. The faculty in the room that day later approached me individually and declared in outraged (but hushed) tones behind their closed office doors, "He outright attacked you! He was actually yelling at you!" and so forth.

The host professor at the Big Ten school introduced me that day to the phenomenon many NAS scholars are all-too familiar with: the "Indian Expert." I had read and heard about this from NAS scholars and Indigenous faculty previously, but had not yet personally experienced it until that unpleasant day. "Indian Experts" are faculty members who appoint themselves as the purveyor of all things Indian on their campuses, though they have no formal education in NAS. These are scholars who have a hobby interest in Indians and develop courses in their departments using the research methodologies and theoretical frameworks of their disciplines, which of course are the colonial narratives about Natives. This may seem like a completely benign endeavor on their part, maybe even an act of Indigenous advocacy, but very often it is not and determining the faculty advocates from the "Indian Experts" is quite easy, though they are often using similar books in their courses, alas. Faculty who are NAS advocates and not "Indian Experts" welcome dialogue, collaboration, and inclusion of NAS scholars. They support the creation of NAS programs on their campuses, include NAS scholars in those decision-making processes (regardless of their faculty rank), develop coursework with us, and in general seek institutional and curricular inclusion of NAS courses and scholars. They see NAS scholars as essential resources. These faculty advocates are key to furthering the work of NAS on American campuses.

However, the "Indian Expert" in her/his role as faculty member is quite different from the NAS Advocate who teaches Native-themed courses in their discipline. The "Expert" is enraged by our presence on campus, attempts (and often succeeds) in sabotaging our endeavors to add NAS courses to university curricula, denigrates our credentials and teaching, challenges our Indigenous identity if we are not tribally enrolled (and even then they still do), and, as much as they can, prevent us from being promoted: denying our bids for tenure or stonewalling promotion of NAS contingency faculty to full-time appointments. These academics put a lot of energy and time into attacking NAS scholars. In sum, the "Indian Experts" are outraged that their colonial ownership of what they deem to be Native knowledge may be displaced on campus by NAS scholars. Very often personal identity plays a role in the "Indian Experts'" sense of entitlement: they believe they are "more Indian" than the NAS scholar or Indigenous faculty member because they spent some vacation time living near/with Indigenous communities when they were undergrads or they personally know Important Indians. Again, this is an act of colonization.

An "Indian Expert" can also be an administrator: they love to show us their collections of Indian artifacts and tell us about their vacation trips to Native-owned casinos and mission trips to reservations. If they learned a few words in an Indigenous language, they will say those few words over and over again whenever the opportunity arises. This is the power of the colonizer, and they are asserting it. When we NAS scholars are not willing to become another silent item in their collection, these administrators can engage in top-down violence by thwarting promotions, excluding us on relevant institutional committees, and by generally promoting a hostile work environment.

What is the solution to the "Indian Experts"? *Ignore them.* Though they are irritating and may even accomplish significant damage to our professional well-being and career trajectory, what I have learned is that, unless we are willing to seek employment elsewhere, we are going to have to re-frame our experience with these co-workers. In the end, they fool no one but themselves, even if they receive institutional accolades.

Discipline-specific harassment of NAS scholars is a direct result of the continued process of colonization. No one gets harassed across the disciplines because they teach Math (unless you are a woman, of course).

Having a graduate degree in Native American Studies carries with it the baggage that *how* and *what* we study is unreliable and illegitimate, and this is used to undermine NAS scholars' authority as scholars, teachers, and experts in our field. Trying to explain this to those outside the discipline can feel like watching Annie Sullivan teaching Helen Keller how to spell water. What I am describing is not a limitation or disability on the part of the learner, but the learner's belief in supremacy, which is the willful refusal to accept that Indigenous peoples in the Americas had in the past and still have today highly-sophisticated cultures in every facet of human expression and structure: governance, art, mathematics, astronomy, storytelling, medicine, spirituality, social networks, sustainable horticultural and agricultural practices, legal systems, and complex record keeping. Here, take my hand, and we'll sign it together: *W-A-T-E-R*.

What it means to teach Native American Studies in higher education is that, simply because of my discipline, let alone my gender and identity, some people will see me as a threat who must be kept on the margins at all costs. Over the years I have had many impromptu conversations with colleagues who gesture for me to step into a stairwell to tell me in whispers and sideways glances to "keep trying" to get my NAS courses added to the curriculum. It seems that at many academic institutions, teaching NAS is equal to instigating a communist takeover; this is because it is not simply one of, but is the core interrogation of, America's interlocking systems of power, privilege, hierarchy and oppression based on conceptualizations of race and gender.

Over the years I have needed campus police protection from

hostile students who physically threatened me, and intervention from university provosts to stop tenured colleagues from denigrating me on campus in front of their entire classrooms of students (*"Sellers is not even qualified to be an adjunct"* and *"What Sellers teaches is bullshit"*). To the people who love Indians as long as they are portrayed as conquered, helpless, and extinct, who invite them to entertain the campus with an annual pow-wow but keep them out of the curriculum, student recruiting data, and faculty ranks, my presence in academia is a source of significant irritation.

This is what Paula was telling me—*"it's not going to be easy."*

Though I certainly experienced the harassment over the past twenty years in academia in a deeply personal way, none of it actually was. Though my stress-level and blood pressure have been dangerously high at times and I have had many dark meltdowns when new crises arose, none of this is about me, at all. What I have personally experienced as a Native American Studies scholar-teacher and a Euro-American woman with Native & Jewish heritages is simply the on-going processes of colonization. Whether someone is calling out to me nonsense in the lunch line (*"Hey Steph, just do a Heyoka on 'em!"*) or making hostile comments right to my face (*"I thought they were all dead?"*), it's all just Yankee Doodle Disorder. When I look at them, I see their black-square hats, white knee-socks, and giant-buckled shoes. They are scared of what I teach, which looks nothing remotely like their schools' Indian mascots or paintings from the first Thanksgiving. Though they are smiling, many of these academics want to make something perfectly clear to me: the Pilgrims and Cowboys won. Indians (and thus my discipline) can only be understood as quaint memories from a distant American (and thus useless) past. The Pilgrims put the decapitated head of Metacom, the son of Chief Massasoit who had helped the earliest settlers of Massachusetts, on a pole after his people saved the new arrivals from starving that first winter. John Wayne shot all the "screechin' savages" and "sent 'em back to the spirit world." After the genocide, those settlers and their descendants wrote the history books that are currently taught in many American institutions of higher learning, and, to them, I have absolutely no right to challenge them. They decide whose testimony is admissible, legitimate, and a valid primary source to understand Indigenous experiences with the Eurosettlers. As the historian definitively claimed on the PBS documentary, the Natives were "just caught in history."

What these positions routinely assert is that the settlers did nothing wrong. Hence the presence of NAS scholars in the academy challenges the colonial, racialized order built into all levels of the American system, especially academia, and thus the presence of a NAS scholar is transgressive and intolerable to the power brokers. The church, academia, and the U.S. government waged a multilateral colonial war against Indigenous peoples in the Americas that continues today. This is what every person's behavior—from the openly hostile host professor at my first job to the vice provost's seemingly benign question about my campus mailbox years ago—were demonstrating to me. Whether they intended it or had any awareness of their social programming or not, every comment marginalized my work, what I represent as a scholar, and was an act of colonization. Their words and actions were a direct result of my performing overt acts of decolonization at those schools.

After these types of blatantly exclusionary, hostile events meant to bully me, assert power over me in the academic hierarchy, or inadvertently express the speaker's belief that to them I clearly do not belong in the campus community, I think of Paula. I remember Paula telling me about the trailer erected on the edge of the University of California at Los Angeles campus in the 1960s that served as the home to one of the first American Indian Studies programs in the country. I think about the pain she felt having her campus office vandalized and priceless traditional objects stolen. I think about what it must have been like for her to make the case, as Frederick Douglas is known to have done for African Americans, that she is placed in the absurd position of arguing that Native Americans are human beings. So, yes, I knew there are other ways to make a living, but I also remember her telling me during our last telephone call before her death that I have a responsibility to enter the fray and teach. She reminded me that I have a duty to the Ancestors, and that I was called to do this work no matter the personal frustrations and attacks. And she reminded me that she was tired, deeply weary and tired from it all, and now it is my turn to do the work alongside all the other NAS scholars in the country (and who I unfortunately only see a few of once a year at a conference).

Understanding that my and many of my NAS colleagues' experiences reflect the continuing colonization of Turtle Island is important. Issues that support that continued colonization include:

1. There are still comparatively few, but the number of academic institutions in the United States that have a Native American Studies program or a NAS department is growing. In 2008 *A Guide to Native American Studies Programs in the United States and Canada* [revised in 2016] reported 130 institutions of higher learning with a NAS program—there are approximately 5,300 total educational institutions in the United States;

2. There is still a dearth of faculty who have a graduate degree in Native American Studies and most institutions in the United States and Canada have no faculty with that educational credential among their faculty ranks. At every institution where I was employed over the past twenty years, I have been the only faculty

member on campus with a Ph.D. in NAS in the history of the school;

3.   Academic curricula in teacher education programs seldom include much, if any, information about Native histories and cultures, which means American teachers are unprepared and unable to teach what many of them very much wish to bring to their students;

4.   Consequently, these individuals who have very little to no knowledge about NAS become college administrators and professors who then, most often unwittingly, teach the colonial narrative to the next generation of students reinforcing a

   cycle of systemic ignorance;

5.   The colonial narrative is embedded in not only the American identity at large but in the various academic disciplines, including their research methodologies, epistemologies, theoretical frameworks, and canonical texts, especially in anthropology and history. Many of the original founders of these disciplines in America openly exploited Indigenous communities and blatantly contradicted Indigenous Elders' transmissions of culture. Some founders of these disciplines went so far as to dig up fresh graves after attending Native funerals, even decapitating the newly-deceased for "research"; hence, the colonial dehumanization process of Natives is built directly into these disciplines.

These realities make what some NAS professors do at American institutions of higher learning very difficult, isolating, and, admittedly, stressful—and *absolutely essential* if America is ever going to move forward in reconstructing the telling of its past into a more accurate and inclusive narrative.

In addition to the lack of institutional representation, there is the compounded problem at institutions geographically located in states that have no federally recognized Indigenous nations or Indigenous communities with whom they could build relationships to support NAS faculty, and importantly, Native students. My experience in Pennsylvania at several academic institutions is, from what I have read in professional journals and heard personally from colleagues, very different from other NAS scholars in the country, and Indigenous peoples in any academic field, in states like California, Kansas, Oklahoma, Minnesota, Washington, and New York where there are highly-visible and engaged Indigenous nations collaborating with educational institutions in their states. The larger universities in Pennsylvania, like the University of Pennsylvania and Penn State, among others, do have NAS programs, but most schools in Pennsylvania do not. This is true for many states in the U.S. Though there are Indigenous communities in Pennsylvania, they do not have the type of representation and institutional partnerships that, for example, the Onondaga nation has at Syracuse University in New York or the Dine people have with the University of Arizona. This leaves Native American Studies scholars and Native American students on their own at most universities, which is a very vulnerable, isolating experience. I still receive blank stares when I say "Native American Studies is its own discipline." A vice president at a large state university once dismissively quipped to me during a discussion about Indigenous inclusion that "Native Americans have such a charming philosophy." To him, I essentially had a doctoral degree in a "charming philosophy."

The message I so often receive about my discipline translates to *"Who cares?"*

Academia aided and abetted European colonization of the

Americas; therefore, academia should be ground-zero for repaying that moral debt by not just "allowing," but proactively fostering inclusion of Indigenous Studies at all levels of engagement: curricular and co-curricular programming, and, most importantly, in student and faculty recruiting and retention efforts. Every Internet landing page of every academic institution in America should clearly state the ancestral lands of the Indigenous peoples on which the school is located and a weblink to local Indigenous cultural information and/or Tribal Councils.

Again, American institutions of higher learning are ground-zero for the work of addressing America's history of Indigenous genocide and land-grabbing. Like all my predecessors in academia before me, and all the people who are doing the same work in their part of the country, I will not stop working for that inclusion. As the Dakota scholar and poet Elizabeth Cook-Lynn declares, it was never just about getting a job as a professor in order to make a living, but was always about taking apart the lies built into American educational curricula about Indigenous histories and cultures. This is what Paula taught me, what my other Native doctoral committee advisor, Barbara Alice Mann, taught me, and what my traditional Native teachers in Pennsylvania taught me since I was a young adult: we can never stop fighting for Indigenous justice. Importantly, we must bring more and more people of all identities into the movement— the earliest Indigenous leaders knew that and though their attempts at building peace and kinship ties with the settlers most often ended in betrayal and disaster, it also ensured the survival of nations that are thriving today: the Mohegan nation in Connecticut is a case in point. When the European settlers arrived, Chief Uncas saw the writing on the birch bark.

The bottomline of what I have learned as a NAS professor is: if you are in Native American Studies, you have to be a fighter.

But as I said, my experience in academia has been one of extremes: from institutional exclusion and hostility to outreach and respect from colleagues to the humbling openness of my students. These past twenty years are heavy with ambiguity, contradiction, grief and fulfillment. Now, here are the joys:

Over the decades I have consistently enjoyed the outreach from long-retired faculty who hear I am on campus and cannot wait to tell me about what they did "back in the day before you were born" to bring Native American histories and cultures into the curriculum. Community leaders, spouses of faculty, alums, and retirees often audit my courses and, from them, meaningful relationships have begun. These folks become not only allies to me, but advocates for Indigenous causes nationally. Some of them are family to me now. And here is a most memorable event: an alumna who had achieved a national position overseeing a branch of the U.S. government visited a university where I was employed. When I thanked her for coming, she asked me what I did at the institution. When I said "teach Native American Studies" she paused, eyes widened, and said "Oh my god" then embraced me. She looked somewhat horrified imagining such an undertaking at that particular school and offered unequivocal recognition for that struggle. Other memories: Indigenous students thanking me for helping them "come out" and "be Indian in public"; former students becoming national and state park guides and bringing the first Indigenous educational programs into those venues against vigorous opposition by their supervisors; faculty colleagues lobbying for inclusion of my NAS courses and making enemies of formerly congenial relationships in the process; seeing more and more students study NAS in graduate school; learning that top-ranking faculty who I barely knew nominated me for promotion.

Best memories: the numerous EuroAmerican male undergrad

students over the years *telling the whole class* how they used to be the guy laughing at people working for the Washington football team's name change or removal of their school's Indian mascots and now they are advocates for those changes. Students who come to me after class and say "I always knew the Earth was sacred" and "We're driving to North Dakota to support the water protectors" and "Sky Woman!? No Way! This just changed my life!!" and "I'm going to be a history teacher now" and "Your class makes me so furious—thank you!" I am extremely proud of them. From these beautiful young people my deepest professional purpose is fulfilled. This is how society changes for the better.

The core issue in my discipline is that a system founded on supremacy is always going to provide opportunities for individuals to express that supremacy if they choose to do so. The answer is not finding "morally pure" people to lead, but to have healthy organizations where there are people who have a body of knowledge about its country's origins and an understanding of the ways colonization is perpetuated today—its tentacles touch everyone, though not equally. Legally requiring the inclusion of Native American histories and cultures in all elementary, secondary, and post-secondary institutions in America is an important way forward. This has already happened in the public school systems of some American states and needs to be nationally instituted as a protocol to get our country out of the Columbian years in American colleges and universities. A decidedly unpopular position, I am certain, but one that is necessary and, in the end, will be to every American's betterment—especially Indigenous peoples'. Doing so would disable the self-appointed "Indian Experts" from waging their wars on NAS scholars because there would be a significant pool of people on campus who know otherwise about Native histories and cultures.

Teacher preparation in Native American histories and cultures is a key component in turning America away from the Columbian mentality. Otherwise, I can see we are decades away from making much progress. NAS scholars like me cannot be subjugated to relying on "the kindness of strangers" in academia in order to have our NAS courses included in the curriculum and taught by qualified faculty. Few institutions would allow an English professor with a fascination in Biology to teach Biology courses; but faculty with no formal education in NAS routinely teach NAS or Native-themed courses in higher education. This only promulgates the colonial narrative.

Paula rose to garner international recognition for her scholarship and leave a lasting legacy, but it came at a very high price. To me and many in her family and community, her death in her sixties was the result of chronic, toxic stress. She paid it for all her students who chose careers in academia because she fought the bitterest first battles so we could get a degree in what became a new discipline called American Indian/Native American Studies. Paula and many other academics of her generation fighting the same fight put a sacred trust in us, the next generation of Indigenous Studies scholars-teachers-artists, to continue the work they started. No matter the challenges before us, we cannot let these Elders down.

Paula angered people within and outside of academia because she dared to weave a different story from the one promulgated in American history books by EuroAmerican settlers about Indigenous peoples. She also angered other Indigenous peoples who did not care for her pointing out the non-colonial versions of their histories and cultural practices in relation to women and queer people—and they lashed out at her in their writings. Paula was unafraid of the margins though, and I believe, befriended those margins, thrived on the margins, and invited many to join her on the margins of the American educational system—even the margins of Indian Country.

Out here on the margins we are all racially and ethnically different and do not often agree about what needs to be done with this settler system that works for but a fraction of the population and that corrupts those for whom it does provide. We are our own community and are using the power of stories. Paula Gunn Allen was one of the many hands who began the weaving of this story in the halls of the Ivory Tower. From *The Woman Who Owned the Shadows* to *The Sacred Hoop* to her final stunning book about Pocahontas (which was nominated for a Pulitzer Prize) she pointed the way for the next generation of Native American Studies scholars. She left touchstones for us to draw strength from during very hard times that inevitably come in this discipline, and she reminds us to laugh and to keep fighting.

As Paula often said, *"She who tells the story rules the world."*

In the end, that is what I do for a living: tell the stories of the Indigenous peoples of Turtle Island as they have crafted, transmitted, and reported them. It is one of the most sacred jobs I can have, and it is a blessing. I made the right decision to become a professor and publish academic books no matter how I have been treated within the system of academia. I have been supported and protected by many faculty colleagues over the years—women and men of all identities have pounded on tables at meetings, written letters to administrators, petitioned, strategized, and took risks, over and over again, to ensure I could teach NAS courses. More and more I see younger colleagues taking sincere interest in teaching components of NAS in their courses, including Indigenous scholarly sources, and entering the academy as professors who have already studied with knowledgeable graduate advisors. Times are changing! These younger faculty inspire me deeply and give me hope—they are also my campus community, which is priceless to me. I believe in their work and their ability to turn the colonial narrative back until it has eaten itself and vanishes.

Teaching NAS under the colonial hailstorm in the academy is one of the most transgressive, radical acts of social transformation in which we can engage.

Professor Auntie Paula and Indigenous Elders in and outside of academia made this possible for me by providing a solid educational foundation grounded in the histories, cultures, epistemologies, and research methodology of Native American Studies. The honorific "Auntie" stems from Indigenous kinship ties and is an acknowledgement of our traditional relationship as family. These Elders not only taught me, but believe in me, a powerful teaching in itself. Paula is now with Iyatiku. Now I am Professor Auntie to the eager students who come into my classroom, and I must continue the great work of those before me: the work of my Cherokee ancestors who were forced at gunpoint by the colonizers to march off their lands on foot; the work of my Sephardic Jewish ancestors who were banished from their homelands century after century; the work of my European-immigrant Appalachian ancestors who continue to be silenced by the societal poisons of elitism and privilege. Their histories and cultures are in me and give me the strength to do this challenging professional work. The blood and bones of my Ancestors are in the Earth where I teach. Some of their names grace the rivers, roadways, histories, and graves in the counties of the schools where I have taught. They hear me. They see me. They cannot be disappeared. When I cross the mountain on my way to work every day, I know many of my people have already made this journey and that they are blessing me now.

Though the acts of colonization meant to victimize me still occur, I have transformed and outrun their ability to harm me a long time ago. I consider all acts of exclusion calls to immediately start writing; that is where I do my fighting.

May my work perpetually honor all my Ancestors and respect the words of the Indigenous nations and Elders I teach. May I fulfill their sacred charge.

Thank you, Auntie. Thank you.

Some Ideas, like Paula's, Endure

The 'Essential' Allen, Two Spirit Identity Politics & Native Literary Nationalism

Sandra Cox

In her "Tribute to Paula Gunn Allen" Annette Van Dyke remarks that Allen was "a major champion" for the "restor[ation of] the place of gay and lesbian Native Americans" in the cultures of tribal nations. Van Dyke notes that Allen worked tirelessly to reclaim and reinvigorate support for spiritual powers of the many Native people fulfilling non-heterosexual roles "for the good of their communities" (70). In fact, one would not be overstating Allen's importance to say that she was among the first to proliferate that idea as a subject of serious academic inquiry and cultural politics. Allen's foundational essay on the subject, "Beloved of Women: Lesbians in American Indian Cultures," was first published in 1981, and was later reprinted in her critical masterwork *The Sacred Hoop*. In that essay she argued that "[t]he lesbian is to the American Indian what the Indian is to the American—invisible" (245). In facing that invisibility, Allen voiced a determination that one needed to "explore lesbianism within a larger social and spiritual tribal context as contrasted with its occurrence as an individual aberration that [. . .] has nothing to do with tribal life in general," and when she herself takes up that exploration, Allen finds that "gayness, whether female or male, traditionally functions positively within tribal groups" (246). The assertion that homophobia in Indigenous cultures is a direct result of colonization supported Allen's potent conviction that reclaiming traditional, life-affirming spiritualties required an embracing of same-sex love and the reestablishment of kinship structures based upon affinity rather than authority. For Allen, critique of and resistance to colonial authority were consistent priorities across identity categories; those institutions that repress women are likely to participate in the oppression of Native Americans and of gays and lesbians. For Allen, the obvious solution was an examination of the interconnectedness of those identities that illuminated more equitable and just ways of living and thinking that are eroded by the systemic and continued imposition of Western ideology. This critical finding—that assumed a gynocentric, nationalistic and queer-positive *a priori* state for many Indian national cultures—shaped Allen's work and influenced the writings of theorists and authors who came after her in profound ways. Because of the expansive nature of the idea, however, it also left her vulnerable to criticism from scholars invested in maintaining a hierarchical relationship between ethnographer and Indigenous subject.

Allen's creative and critical work serves as an incipient point for Two-Spirit studies and movements. In Will Roscoe's acknowledgements in the first anthology of literature and critical works "compiled by gay American Indians" in 1986 (the same year in which *The Sacred Hoop* is first published), Allen is the first individual thanked by name. In fact, Roscoe chose to open Part One of the text by printing Allen's poem "Some like Indians Endure" (9). While Allen was a prolific, talented, relevant and accomplished author in more than one genre, this particular poem serves as an example of her expansive and innovative expression of Two-Spirit consciousness. The poem begins "i have it in my mind that / dykes are Indians /

they're a lot like Indians" (9). This statement—and the alliance between non-Native queers and Native Americans it posits—implies a radically inclusive politics of identity that bridges ethnicity and sexuality. That implicit politics is relevant across cultural communities, political movements and academic disciplines. Allen denies any argument in favor of mimesis by the titular Indians—after all the "some" are "like Indians," but Allen never argues that the "Indians" are like "some." As the referent to which an analogue is attached, "Indians" are an original rather than a copy, simulation or construction. Additionally, the opening three lines stress the subjective space that the narrator speaking the lines occupies. By beginning in the mind of that narrator, Allen marks a conceptual possibility rather than a concrete truth. The shifts between the second and third lines—from the metaphor to the simile—point out that an identification between "dykes" and "Indians" is immediately revised to an analogy between "dykes" and "Indians." By stressing similarities and shared experiences across ethnic boundaries, Allen creates a space for political alliances of affect between the two categorically oppressed groups. Allen's poem—like much of her critical work—suggests that experiences of oppression can become spaces for developing allegiance. The poem calls for identification across differences and coalition without colonization.

Allen depicts clear connections between the Two-Spirit consciousness and a new politics of identity; these connections are of particular interest when one examines the ways in which her work has been framed in recent debates between nationalist and cosmopolitanist scholars who wish to guide practices for reading Native-authored literature. On the one hand, cosmopolitanist critics find Allen's work too devoid of high theory and too dismissive of Euro-American influences and confluences on Native literary and cultural studies. Nationalist critics, on the other hand, defend the preferential treatment that Allen gives to Native cultural, historical and literary antecedents. There are a number of examples of this contention about Allen's work, but the accusations of essentialism that critic Elvira Pulitano leveled against Allen in the book *Toward a Native American Critical Theory* incited the largest amount of controversy. Pulitano's arguments are a clear (albeit exaggerated) exemplification of the sort of critique that *The Sacred Hoop* has elicited from cosmopolitanists. In the second chapter of *American Literary Nationalism* Craig Womack, Robert Warrior and Jace Weaver note that Pulitano's critique of Allen's methods is "focused on the way in which Allen pits Native cultures against the totalized western Other as the center of her study, that is the oppositional mode Allen writes in insists on Indian purity versus a corrupted European legacy" (Womack, Weaver and Warrior 164-5). Actually, Allen's work is quite the opposite. Instead of unfairly criticizing Western ideology as a monolith, Allen presents a nuanced analysis of the ways in which culture, gender and sexual orientation function as evidence of particular colonialist, patriarchal and homophobic ideologies. Her analysis emanates from an investigation of discrete, distinct and direct acts of institutional oppression. Allen then documents instances of that oppression through her own creative work and through her scholarly investigations of the work of other Native writers.

Allen's critical and literary work reconstructs non-heterocentric Native cultural and literary productions, and repudiates the rejection of queer identity in non-Native cultures without totalizing. The impulse to totalize, Allen has argued, comes from outsider critics who reorder Native traditions to resemble Western antecedents:

> According to ethnographers' accounts among the tribes there were women warriors, women leaders, women shamans, women husbands, but whether any of these were lesbians is seldom mentioned. [. . .] This fosters the impression of

uniform heterosexuality among Indian women. [. . .] It is an impression which is false. (*The Sacred Hoop* 245).

The construction of an ethnosexual norm occurs in the act of literary colonization that accompanies the transcription by the ethnographer. This claim does not romanticize a pre-contact utopia of Indian cohesion and harmony, rather it acknowledges that the information available about the pre-contact conditions of Native communities is unreliable at best and overtly hostile to Two-Spiritism at worst because of the predilections of the scholars gathering the information for posterity. Allen implies that the best way to grapple with this unreliable information from ethnographic criticism of folklore and literary production is to replace it with autoethnography.

When the cultural landscape is described by a speaking subject immersed in the cultural landscape—like Allen's own voice in her novel, autobiography, poetry and interviews—then, quite a different story is told. Rather than serving as informant to an ethnographer who draws conclusions without context, the use of an autoethnographic lens to understand lore allows for a more expansive reparative view on Native national cultures. Allen's own revisions of her Scottish uncle's ethnographic work on the Keres at the Laguna pueblo demonstrate that a great deal of work is required to find the intersections underneath the reinscription of colonial perspectives:

I'm beginning to be able to take the Laguna stories that my uncle, John Gunn, printed in his book *Schat-cher*—he did very odd things to those stories. I know enough about Laguna people and Laguna ritual that I'm beginning to be able to say what he did. [. . .] He masculinizes. He made it European and patriarchal; he made it hierarchical and elitist,

even though Lagunas are neither, and he attempted to make
us look like European people, which is no help to us. No help
to me as a writer, and it's no help to the people as a people.
It's just a useless exercise. But I'm beginning to be able to
unscramble it and say, 'Well look. All he got was a story from
somebody that was about a dance. And they were telling him
what the dance was about. That's all they were doing.' And he
turned it into a nice little northern European fairy tale. [. . . .
I]f he had told it as it was meant in the context from which it
arises, then there would have been a better understanding of
what it is that particular ritual is about, and what it is these
people are doing. It would have been told in a very congenial
way that people could understand. (Ballinger and Swann 9).

As she recontextualizes Gunn's ethnographic work the bias she
finds becomes more apparent and the mechanisms by which the
lore might be more appropriately understood are proliferate and
multivalent. In multiplying cultural meaning without totalizing a
Western other (note that she does not accuse Gunn, but rather
traces his own cultural modes of interpreting that make a Keres
ritual into a European fairy tale), Allen implies an identity politics
that neither manufactures an Indian essence (which cosmopolitanists find distasteful) nor embraces a "hybridity" that suggests
that Native identity inevitably is tainted or permuted by colonial
power (which nationalists find reprehensible). In place of these
polarized ways of examining cultural purity or permeability, Allen
posits a decolonial imagining—a way of understanding how colonial power distorts identity through ideology and narrative. This
decolonization of the text that creates many possible stories from
one ethnographic record constitutes a form of autoethnographic
criticism and authorship that finds spaces that are overwritten by
colonial power. Allen's project is a radical reversal of the colonial
palimpsest that she finds in *Schat-cher*, instead of overwriting, she

attempts to peel back layers of narrative frame and to find patterns and sense in the pastiche and fragments that point to a specific cultural ideology that is neither pure nostalgia for an unattainable cultural incipience nor is it a sad ballad written to commemorate the end of the proverbial trail for the Keres people.

Allen's work reveals a new identity politics. In the same interview in which she describes how the study of lore informs her reparative readings of ethnographic texts, Allen states that her work is "speaking out of a lesbian consciousness [. . .] out of a gynocratic consciousness that, as it happens, lesbians somewhat share" with some Native nations (6). The use of gender and sexuality as a mechanism for shared consciousness is further examined in her poetry. Allen implicitly argues for an understanding garnered from Native traditions that crafts a political, social and multicultural alliance across ethnic, gendered and sexual identities. Returning to my earlier discussion of the poem that opens Roscoe's anthology, I notice that "Some Like Indians [. . .]" explains the reasons why non-Native queers are like Native Americans in terms that reify the claims Allen makes in *The Sacred Hoop* and in those interviews about her decolonial archival revisions. The narrator of the poem continues,

because they bear
witness bitterly
because they reach
and hold
because they live every day
with despair laughing
in cities and country places
because earth hides them
because they know
the moon (10)

The shared experience of institutional oppression and daily struggles for survival unifies lesbians and Native Americans without making claims to mimicry, hierarchy or exclusivity. Both dykes and Indians testify to the colonial oppression writ large upon their experiences. Both dykes and Indians know how joy in community can temper the despair of systemic violence and ideological erasure. Both dykes and Indians know that a diasporic divide, making some of them urban and some rural, is a mechanism for preventing solidarity and resistance, and in spite of that division "they gather together/enclosing /and spit in the eye of death" (10). Allen's poetic work, which like Indians and dykes has occasionally been ignored and devalued, on Two-Spirit identity is so very important because scholars of Two-Spirit identity that come after her are "more interested in learning Native categories of reality than imposing those developed in Western social and other sciences" (Jacobs 27) because of her introduction of this line of analysis.

Allen creates space in her writing; she hypothesizes that collective action and cross-ethnic understandings are possible without neglecting the specificity of cultural difference. In a short note in *Signs*, Beth Brant argued that "being a Native lesbian is like living in the eye of a hurricane—terrible, beautiful, filled with sounds and silences, the music of life-affirmation and the disharmony of life-despising" (944). Allen's writings set those sounds—both musical and disharmonious—down in words and in doing so her poetry and her critical work created the rhetorical space in which ideological resistance to colonial power could grow.

Because Allen's work on lesbianism in Native cultures and literatures illuminates the inseparability of gender from sex, sexuality, race, ethnicity and national origin, the notion of social justice initiatives organized around sexual preference and gender identity became a desirable of Pan-Indian movements. After all, like "Indian" and "Queer," "Two-Spirit" is an umbrella term; it encompasses many ways of being and varied traditions and cultural practices.[21] Native peoples' different understandings of gender, sex and sexuality may have been subsumed in some ways by the western binaries between male and female and masculine and feminine. However, a full continuum of identities for some tribal communities continues to be preserved and respected. For Allen (and those who follow her), it was important to note that these differentiated cultural understandings are just as likely to construct equally rigid rules regarding gender-crossing and, on occasion, may have allowed cross-gender performances but not homosexuality. In fact, Allen's own work demonstrates a concern for how tradition might be misrepresented or misunderstood by outsiders seeking to appropriate Two-Spirit identities for their own ends. Again, discussing her work on Keres lore, Allen notes that "Lagunas are a heavily 'mother right' culture. I won't call it matriarchal, because that means something real bizarre in English, that no Indian ever dreamed of, believe me" (Ballinger and Swann 5-6). Because she recognizes that some people may misunderstand the ways in which she presents her claims about the social system she is researching, Allen is exceedingly careful to unpack connotative meaning so that reductive understandings of Laguna culture as oppositionally related to Western heteropatriarchy are complicated rather than facile. Allen does not want readers to reinscribe a new hierarchy in place of that old one, but rather she notes that privileging "mother rights" does not necessitate women's dominance of men the way patriarchal systems perpetuate men's dominance of women. Allen's work is among the earliest Native-authored criticism to make note of these varied traditions and to begin revise ethnographic readings of those culturally derived understandings. Anishnawbe anthropologist Midnight Sun was

---

21 Some of my explication of the ways the term "Two-Spirit" has been used can also be found in my contribution to the volume *Louise Erdrich: Critical Perspectives*.

another, who argued that "a lack of information regarding Indigenous ideologies makes analysis difficult, but certain hypotheses may be made by attempting to situate native sex/gender systems in contexts specific to their societies" (Roscoe 45). Because Allen's work has begun a conversation about these issues the ways in which Midnight Sun and others are able to explain the terms of this debate about the role of hegemony and sexuality in producing misreadings of cultural norms without committing the totalizations of which the cosmopolitanists find Allen guilty.

Even though Allen was not part of the movement that coined the term Two-Spirit, her work presented a vacuum into which the kind of work scholars who did could posit a theoretical foundation that necessitated a new terminology. "Two-Spirit" is necessarily aspecific with regard to tribal origin, which is why it is not translated into any Native language (Jacobs et al. 276-278). Like Allen's theoretical perspective, Two-Spiritism is *both* relevant in a cosmopolitanist context—it eschews national specificity in favor of Pan-Indian concerns—*and* powerfully nationalistic—it repudiates the transference of EuroAmerican norms to Indigenous cultural contexts. The term expresses many sexual, social and familial roles—from men who love men, to women who live as men, to sacred clowns who enact both genders fluidly, and many other identities besides—and all these performances are derived from a tradition of variant expressions of gender identity within many tribal histories. Two-Spirit is quite different from queer in that way; queer denotes a deviation from a rigidly defined norm, but Two-Spirit suggests a performance outside the masculine/feminine-male/female dichotomies that is not an aberration but a celebrated and crucial fulfillment of a set of traditional Native American roles (Jacobs et. al. 287). Allen demonstrates that the ways in which Queer activism attempted to shift the ideology behind sex/gender systems were retrofitted to traditional beliefs of many Indian nations. The affinity between GLBTQ peoples and some Indigenous groups was there—because both communities were committed to resisting a compulsory heterosexuality that was enforced with genocidal violence within a series of repressive institutions.

Furthermore, the revision of "white feminism" that Native women and queer theorists struggle with generates more continuity among their positions. Allen has noted that "most of the Indian women I know have been hurt by white feminism and have a very ambivalent feeling toward it" (Ballinger and Swann 6). In spite of the trepidation about extraethnic solidarity between women, Allen, in *The Sacred Hoop*, details the ways in which the political project that second wave liberal feminism undertook in the United States owes much to the matrilineal, gynocentric cultural values of many southwestern Indigenous cultures. The argument she makes about the role of Native women's interventions in feminist theory and literary criticism is well-covered in the critical conversation about her work, and those interventions have much in common with the ways she implicitly intervenes in queer theory and activism through the "lesbian consciousness" she locates in her writing. In Western culture queer people are marginal; in Indigenous cultures two-spirit people were often central. Likewise, EuroAmerican patriarchy marginalizes women and centralizes men. As Allen encouraged the white feminists that her Native women friends turned away from to see the interventions in gender politics and ethnic politics as linked, her work on sexuality in Indigenous cultural systems is also intersectional with those political concerns.

In Allen's work the separation of men from women, of Natives from non-Natives, of "straights" from "queers" is an ideological illusion—she stresses interconnectedness and interreliance. However to note that identity-based difference is ideologically produced and therefore illusory did not stop Allen from investigating the ways in which systemic racism, sexism and homophobia constrain lived experiences. This argument, it might be said, is somewhat akin to Kwame Anthony Appiah's compelling argument that "race" is illusory as a physical or biological fact because the concept only has material import in the socio-cultural construction of racial identity. Just as the illusory nature of race does not make it any easier for Appiah, when accompanied by Houston Baker and Henry Louis Gates, Jr., to hail a cab in Harlem in the late nineties, the repressed cultural prestige of Two-Spiritism does little to prevent gaybashing and feminism does not eradicate cultural chauvinism.[22] Sexual identity, and the cultural caché or stigma that might accompany it, are only ideas, but they are ideas that often influence the lived experience of the people who embody them. What is at stake is not just the stuff of self-actualization—our ideas of who we are—but also the ascription of pruriency to those ideas and our somatic embodiment of them, which put people of color, people of non-heterosexual orientations and women at risk of violence, erasure or exclusion. Allen's "Some like Indians" reminds her readers of the force of an idea of self:

indian is an idea
some people have of themselves
dyke is an idea
some women have of themselves
the place where we live now is idea
because whitemen took
all the rest
because father
took all the rest
but the idea which

22 For a complete context of the "taxi fallacy" see Gates's *Loose Canons*

once you have it
you can't be taken
for somebody else (10)

In this poem, as in Allen's critical work, the re-inscription of Two-Spirit identity is a powerful idea. The parallels of the two communities are inscribed as points of coalescing contact that have potential for ideological and political reclamation. Just as "dyke" identity cannot be erased by the patriarchal institutions communicated by Allen's invocation of "father," "indian" identity cannot be erased by the colonial institutions communicated by her invocation of "whitemen." The idea of what one is—the self-determination of identity—is the only means Allen presents of self-preservation or of communal belonging. Those ideas, in turn, become a geographic space, "the place where we live now," which calls to mind the sort of emphatic focus on land ownership and treaty rights that Native communities face or the kind of exclusions from fair housing and marriage rights that lesbians face. Because the antecedent for the pronoun "we" is unclear—is it "dykes" or "indians"?—the collusion between the two groups is formed grammatically as well as politically and poetically.

Allen's work has become part of a conversation about intersections of gender, sexuality and cultural origins. When nationalist critics have framed her work—and sometimes the resulting conversation—Allen is accused of prioritizing gendered or sexual politics over the issues that frame discourses of national identity for Native peoples. Allen responds that "I don't think my preoccupation with the importance of women is a result of being gay" (Ballinger and Swann 11), and argues that if anything the "woman-centered" traditions of her ethnic background may have contributed to her sexuality, which is "not a political choice" but an idea of who she (6). Allen's use of enjambment in the final line of the preceding quotation is important. Those who claim their own ideas of themselves "can't be taken / for somebody else." The double-entendre of "taken"—as both an instance of captivity and as a euphemism for heteromasculinist sexuality—works to highlight cultural histories of land theft, child removal, and continuing struggles against sexual violence for Indian populations and lesbian women. The line break between the verb phrase and the preposition that begins the dependent clause calls for readers to pause between "you can't be taken" and "for somebody else." This pause is pregnant with possibility, and it makes the person who possesses this idea of him or herself impenetrable. Often, the consequences of Two-Spirit identity in a homophobic colonial system like the contemporary U.S. is that the perceptibly "queer" body is subject to being taken—physically, psychically and sexually.[23]

Two-Spirit people have been institutionalized in order to be "cured of their mental illness" and, like all those who transgress against the compulsory nature of heterosexuality in EuroAmerican civilizations, they face threats of rape and assault because of their "deviant" ideas of themselves. Qwo-Li Driskill, a Native nationalist, queer theorist and poet, has noted that "[s]exual assault is an explicit act of colonization that has enormous impacts on both personal and national identities and because of its connections to a settler mentality, can be understood as a colonial form of violence and oppression" (50-62). In considering how personal experiences of sexual violation are connected to a cultural history of land theft, limited sovereignty and overt genocide, Driskill posits that sexual violence and gender proscription are tools that are regularly used to force Indigenous peoples to abandon their own traditions. The

---

23 Additional consideration of the problem of sexual violence as continued colonization can also be found in my contribution to *Bodies and Culture: Discourses, Communities, Representations, Performances*.

relationship that is constructed in mainstream culture between gender and sexual desire forges an implicit link between western heteronormativity and sexual violence against those whose identities are constructed as marginal. After the possibility of protection from that violent taking is removed by the end of the pause indicated by the line break in "Some like Indians," Allen gives a prepositional phrase that points out that what "can't be taken" is not the body, but the identity. The subject who has the idea of him or herself cannot be taken for "somebody else;" Allen suggests that a reclamation of that idea from colonial authority can prevent erasure through assimilation or cultural imperialism even if corporeal violation and institutional violence cannot be averted. When considering that the "idea / some people have of themselves" is all that stands between Two-Spiritism and the successful eradication of Native cultural traditions regarding sex, gender and sexuality, Allen's poem, and its implicit call for interethnic alliances to work toward ending homophobia as a means of controlling identity, should be as important as the debates between cosmopolitanism and nationalism. The ways she follows up on that powerful pair of lines presents the deliberative impetus clearly for readers:

everybody is related
to everybody
in pain
in terror
in guilt
in blood
in shame
in disappearance
that never quite manages
to be disappeared

The fusing of lesbian and Native experience is not just about suffering—pain, terror, guilt, blood and shame—but also about resilience and the refusal "to be disappeared." It is that infinite and irascible feature that means that "everybody is related / to everybody else." Driskill makes note of the ways in which rape is part of the colonial practice that attempts erasure, and Allen, who began the critical conversation in which Driskill is participating, notes that the failure of several centuries of sexual violence to affect that erasure becomes a foundation for solidarity.

Just as Allen's theoretical work and Driskill's critique of sexual violence share an emphasis on reclaiming the lost sacred potential of Two-Spirit people, so does their poetry share a vision for alliance across ethnic differences. Driskill's collection, *Walking with Ghosts*, contains a handful of poems that are literary enactments of mourning from within the GLBTQ community that portray a sense of solidarity across identity-based differences that is quite similar to Allen's perspective in "Some like Indians." For instance, the poem "For Marsha P. (Pay It No Mind!) Johnson" begins with an epigraph drawn from Joy Harjo's elegy "For Anna Mae Pictou Aquash." Aquash was allegedly murdered by FBI agents for her participation in the American Indian Civil Rights Movement. Marsha Johnson was a drag queen found floating in the Hudson after NYC Pride; the NYPD insisted that her death was either suicide or an accident. By suggesting that Aquash's murder is an analogue for Johnson's, Driskill's poem works to expose public complicity in the silence surrounding both deaths, and to suggest that this silence contributes to ongoing violence against all systemically oppressed populations. That Allen's argument that "dykes / are like indians" has been taken up by Driskill is evidence of the long-reaching force of her writing and thinking. I do not, however, mean to suggest that Allen's participation in this discourse was only as a foremother for critics like Driskill. Even in her final illness, her work seemed to contribute to the conversation that Driskill exemplifies above. For instance her last, posthumously published collection contained a sequence of several poems entitled "America the Beautiful." In many ways, these poems respond to the issues raised by Driskill in *Walking with Ghosts*. In particular, Driskill's concrete poem "Map of the Americas," which figures a Native person speaking to his or her non-Native lover as if the body of the beloved was Indian country and lovemaking an act of colonialism, has some important antecedents reflected in "America the Beautiful IX," in which Allen's narrator speaks about the U.S. as an Indian woman who is becoming whiter as time progresses: "as though crazed / that ancient dame / created chemicals dangerous to herself so we / could vilify their use / and there find our own redemption" (19). I could not say if Allen was reading Driskill's work as she faced her final illness and penned these lines. Even if she did not, and was unable to stay current with the movement in the field she helped to create and define, the prescience with which she imagines a rejoinder to Driskill's permissive beloved, who allows the non-Native lover to possess her bodily, by considering how a fourth term—the land itself—might be added to the discursive construction of sexuality, gender and ethnicity through Native literature.

In conclusion, Allen's own final stanzas to "Some Like Indians" might even be instructions for those considering how to respond to the theoretical and literary calls-to-action her work conveyed. She stresses the responsibility people have to one another and the desperate strength of the ideas we hold of ourselves:

we never go way
even if we're always
leaving

because the only home
is each other
they've occupied all
 the rest
colonized; an
idea about ourselves is all
we own (12)

What Allen bequeathed to feminist literary theory, Native American literary studies and gender and sexuality studies is this new idea about "ourselves"—all of us allied in ideological activism through scholarship and literature—that is radically inclusive yet intensely culturally specific, because those qualities define her intellectual, artistic and activist projects. It is a legacy that we must all endeavor to preserve.

Interview With Dr. Lisa Tatonetti

Menoukha R. Case & Stephanie A. Sellers

Dr. Tatonetti, first of all, we want to thank you for taking the time to communicate with us via email about the work of Paula Gunn Allen. Considering your 2014 book The Queerness of Native American Literature, *you are well-positioned to provide important insights on Allen's influences in the fields of Native American Literary Studies and Two-Spirit Studies.*

1. When did you first read Paula Gunn Allen's writing, which piece was it, and what impact did it have on you?

I first read Paula Gunn Allen around 1993. I was a non-traditional student returning to school when I took an honors seminar on Native American Women's literature that changed the course of my life. Among many other important texts, we read Allen's edited collection, *Spider Woman's Granddaughters*. I still remember how Allen's powerful return to the Pueblo Yellow Woman stories—especially the way she layered the traditional "collected" stories together with her own and Leslie Silko's retellings—opened up my understanding of story cycles and oral narratives and Indigenous perspectives. I read *The Sacred Hoop* on my own that semester, which introduced me to tribal feminisms and to the often-radical difference between the perspectives of mainstream and Indigenous feminisms. I still teach that section of *Spider Woman's Granddaughters* in my introductory Native literature courses and, nearly thirty years after that collection was originally published, Allen's work introduces students to the complex nature of Indigenous storytelling and knowledge production more effectively than almost anything I know.

2. Allen's earliest scholarly and creative works are heavily referenced in your 2014 book The Queerness of Native American Literature. *Would you talk about the role these works played in the formation of Two-Spirit Studies and your work within that field?*

Paula Gunn Allen spoke out and spoke up about the intersections of queerness and Indigeneity at a time when such ties were not openly discussed. There's a reason why both *Living the Spirit*, the first collection of queer Indigenous literature, which was published in 1989 and *Sovereign Erotics*, the most recent collection of queer Native literature, both begin with Allen's poem "Some Like Indians Endure." Allen's provocative opening, "I have it in my mind that / dykes are Indians // they're a lot like Indians" pushes at the boundaries, at the intersections, of Two-Spirit identities by claiming affiliations that made some folks uncomfortable. She did the same thing in her novel *The Woman Who Owned the Shadows* by giving us a queer Indigenous protagonist who finds healing in the power of the erotic. Likewise, *The Sacred Hoop* staked claims for gender diversity among Indigenous nations and opened up conversations about Two-Spirit identities well before they were happening in the field. My understanding is that Allen brought conversations about queer Indigeneity to the table at the 1977 NEH Flagstaff meeting where she was project director. So from the very first, not only at the meeting that's often cited as the beginning of American Indian literary studies, but also in all aspects of her work, Allen refused to allow heteronormative readings of Native literatures and cultures to exist unchallenged.

3. *You write in* The Queerness of Native American Literature *that "the critical reception of Allen's text [*Studies in American Indian Literatures*] can be read as a narrative of a field becoming." We could not agree with you more, and* Weaving the Legacy *is our testament to this belief. That said, do you believe Allen is sufficiently included in conversations literary scholars have about the field of Native American literature today? If not, how is she positioned, and why?*

I ABSOLUTELY do not think Allen is sufficiently included in conversations about Native American literature. Allen's interventions into Indigenous studies are both creative and scholarly. She wrote important literature, she crafted a scholarly field, and she worked tirelessly to do so. Allen was a rule breaker and an innovator. Stephanie Fitzgerald shared a story I love about TA-ing for Allen in a UCLA course on vampire literature. How many years was this before the vampire craze? Allen was just one of those folks who pushed ahead fearlessly.

Allen is not just a "first," however. I might get in trouble from Callahan scholars here, but her work is not like *Wynema*, a text we teach and laud because of its position as the first known novel by an Indigenous woman even though the text itself is a bit of a trainwreck. Allen was breaking ground, was opening up conversations, was pushing all these "firsts" in creating Native American literary studies as a field, in writing Two-Spirit literature, in offering queer Indigenous critiques, in writing book-length scholarly criticism on Native literature, AND she was writing simply brilliant poetry and scholarship. There are so many examples. Pieces like "Pocahontas, to Her English Husband, John Rolfe" come to mind here.

4. *Would you address the criticism that Allen was an "essentialist"?*

How would I address the criticism that Allen was essentialist? I would say, yes, Allen was at times essentialist. Aren't we all? Aren't so many Indigenous writers and scholars? Take N. Scott Momaday's famous claim "An Indian is an idea a man has of himself." That statement is terribly essentialist. First, there is *an* Indian identity. Second, that Indian identity is singularly male. Yet, at the same time, in the same piece, Momaday tells a specifically Kiowa story and privileges an Indigenous woman as a key purveyor of Indigenous knowledge. I could offer so many examples like this; however, you don't often hear Momaday spoken of with derision. And frankly, especially from younger scholars, I've heard many folks dismiss Allen. I've heard her name coupled with "new age" and "crazy." Many of those folks have never even read her. There's a deep misogyny at work in that sort of easy dismissal.

Allen had a wide-ranging intellect and a mind that was open to alternative possibilities. Those possibilities sometimes took her to places where she discussed crystal skulls and a kind of monolithic matrilinealism among Indigenous peoples—these are the two areas for which I've most often seen her critiqued. I'm not going to try and debunk those critiques. I instead want to say she was and is so much more than that. In many ways, she defines Indigenous futurisms in her ability to imagine differently. She was able to imagine a world in which queer Indigenous histories were acknowledged and contemporary LGBTQ/Two-Spirit people could move freely in the world, embracing an Indigenous erotic as a space of power rather than shame. She was able to imagine a world in which the power of Indigenous literatures was recognized by more than just a select few readers. She imagined differently, expansively,

5. What would you say is Allen's legacy?

In many ways, Allen's legacy IS Native American literary studies. She worked tirelessly for a space in which Indigenous literatures would be read, taught, and respected. She was pivotal to the creation of the field: she ran workshops, led meetings, and sat on editorial boards; she edited key collections and advocated for Indigenous women writers more broadly; she wrote important creative work as well as the first book of literary criticism. Moreover, her words have served as lifelines to Native peoples who didn't see their experiences reflected anywhere. Overall, Allen returned extant Indigenous knowledges to light and built frameworks for new understandings of Indigenous literatures as a whole and for Native feminisms specifically. In the end, Allen's importance cannot be overstated.

At the Edge of Reality

Kristina Bitsue

Summer was furious with temperatures
scorching. The effects of global warming
has tampered with the obvious.
I don't know how grandmother

tracked her souls through the
ashy sands with very little water,
preoccupied with the chasing shadow
of her sheepherder's stick in poise. The
weather vitalizes another story

as she lifted the corral gate shut. Bits
and pieces of wealth have been scattered
under the sun driven clouds while the
birthing of the evening horizon follows

a passing siesta of falling cedar.
Curtains blanket wrinkles of junctions
inside the clouds, while they scramble together
preparing for an announced gale. The
Gods sent along the rain to deluge the terrain

but failed to realize who would awaken. So
they sprinkled some moisture -- here and there, just
enough for the dogs to find shelter under
grandfather's old tractor, an outdated machine
only used to repair the arteries of *Oak Mesa*

Road after the gushing rainstorms. My
Grandmother appeared, unnoticed, from behind
the shed, startling the sheep dogs. Scolding them
for their laziness, she demanded *New York's* return
to foster the flock. His ears set down backward,

his tail tucked between his legs, he chased a crossing
whirlwind beyond the woodpile. Laughing at the dog,
she placed her *giish* against the cemented wall and
entered the house. Sitting on her one-seat couch she
loosened the string from her bonnet and set it

down, cursing the day's heat. Later at the doorway
she ensured the safety of the herd and greeted
a frog. Frustrated with her exhaustion she located
her *tadidiin* bag, pinched into the empty corners
with her fingertips, shoveling yellow corn pollen
with her nails.

She spoke to the frog softly through prayer
asking for rain, forgiveness, and more rain. In her
thoughts she remembered the slumbering crops
have yet to be nourished within the surrounding
arroyos of the desolate fields. Water levels
dropped substantially this year. The

chapter house increased their costs for water,
implementing limitations again. The posting of
the sign leaves us all stunned:

<u>No</u> **washing your hair on Tuesdays**, *You*
can only drink Kool-aid at the dormitory; but
most importantly, use only one-fourth a cup
of water for ceremonial purposes. Have a nice
day!

Is it being over exaggerated? Most likely
not. *Shimasan* did not flinch when she
sprinkled pollen on the frog's back. She only
looked up into the restless heavens and witnessed
the collision of wrestling clouds. The sprinklers

were turned on and salivated down onto the land,
only to fill empty water tanks and a water barrel
used for homemade showers. The drops painted the
faded tractor as the frogs emerged from the moistened
sands, croaking out their freedom into the night.

The next day she stood at the mouth of the house
cursing the rain. She needed to take the
sheep out before noon. Her daily tasks were already
scheduled in her palm pilot. My *cheii* scolded
her for her doings but she had no complaints as

the coldness tapped against her skin. The blue jays jetted
between the rainbow beings. Grandmother's hands
were spooned into the moistened earth, peppering a sand
painting of her own Beauty Way to correct her doings.

Global warming mobs the cosmos and invited space
and time enter the puzzle. The frog returned
to slumber beneath the stormy depths of chaos and
frustration. And in a glimpse we realized that we
are all at the edge of reality.

Remembering Paula Gunn Allen
(1939–2008)

A. LaVonne Brown Ruoff

How do you say farewell to a dear friend of thirty-one years? My mind turns to memories of all our conversations and experiences together over three decades.[24] Born on 24 October 1939, in Albuquerque, Paula Marie Francis was the daughter of Ethel Haines Gottlieb ("Tu'u'we'tsa," "like a song") and Elias Lee Francis II. Her mother was Laguna, Métis, and Scottish while her father was Lebanese American. Her relatives spoke Arabic, English, Laguna (Keres), German, and Spanish and practiced Catholicism, Presbyterianism, and Lutheranism. Raised as a Catholic, she received some of her elementary education at St. Joseph Mission School, San Fidel, administered by the Sisters of Saint Frances. At age seven, she entered Saint Vincent Academy, where she boarded from 1946 to 1951. Operated by the Sisters of Charity, Saint Vincent Academy was located in Albuquerque. In seventh grade, she returned to St. Joseph. Paula went back to Saint Vincent in 1942 as an eighth-grade, day student, graduating in 1957. Saint Vincent's was primarily a college-preparatory high school for

---

24 An earlier version of this eulogy was published in *A Usable Past: Tradition in Native North American Arts and Literatures*, ed. Simone Pellerin, Bordeaux: Presses Universitaires, 2010.

girls.[25] During this period she lived in Albuquerque with her paternal grandfather, Narcesse Francis.

After graduation, Paula attended Colorado Women's College from 1957 to 1958, when she left to marry Eugene Hanosh, a Lebanese American. After giving birth to Lauralee and Eugene John, she divorced Hanosh in 1962. Paula then entered the University of Oregon, where she received her B.A. in English in 1966. She married Darrel Brown, a non-Indian from Kansas, in 1964. Brown adopted both Lauralee and Eugene, who took his name. After divorcing Brown in 1971, Paula married Joe Charles Allen, an Oklahoma Cherokee, in 1972. During this marriage, she bore twins, Suleiman and Fuad Ali. The latter died of crib death as an infant. The couple divorced in 1975.[26]

25 Information from Sister Consolata, principal of St. Joseph Mission School (now closed). Paula says in "A *MELUS* Interview: Paula Gunn Allen" that she went to school in Cubero and San Fidel. Sister Consolata says there never was a mission school in Cubero. Telephone conversation, 18 November 2009. Information on Paula's years at Saint Vincent Academy (1884-1969) provided by Susan M. Murphy, superintendent of Catholic Schools, Archdiocese of Santa Fe. Email 14 December 2009.

26 Information from Lauralee Brown Hannes daughter of Paula Gunn Allen. Emails: 3 November and 23 November 2009.

Allen, Paula Gunn. "*Yo Cruozo Siete Mares*: Paula Frances Allen and E. Lee Frances." *La Confluencia* 1.2 (1976):14-22. Rpt. *Off the Reservation: Reflections on Boundary–Busting, Border-Crossing Loose Cannons*. Boston: Beacon,1998.193-206

Ballinger, Franchot, and Brian Swann, eds. "A *MELUS* Interview: Paula Gunn Allen." *MELUS* 10.2 (1983):3-25.

Coltelli, Laura, ed. "Paula Gunn Allen." *Winged Words: American Indian Writers Speak*. Lincoln: U of Nebraska P, 1990.10-39.

Marquez, Letisia. "Obituary: Paula Gunn Allen, 68, noted English, American Indian studies scholar." University of California, Los Angeles. Newsroom (7 June 2008). http://www.newsroom.ucla.edu/ucla/obituary-paula-gunn-allen-68-noted-51516.aspx

"Paula Gunn Allen Online Memorial." http://www.paulagunnallen.net

In 1968, Paula received a M.F.A. in creative writing from the University of Oregon. By l976, she had earned a Ph.D. in American Studies from the University of New Mexico. After her last marriage ended, Paula not only coped with the difficulties of raising her children alone and studying for her graduate degrees but also with her growing realization that she was lesbian. Later she had several long-term relations with women, including the poet Judy Grahn.

During her academic career, Paula taught at Fort Lewis College, Colorado; The College of San Mateo; San Diego State University; San Francisco State University; and University of New Mexico. Subsequently, she became professor of Native American and ethnic studies at the University of California, Berkeley. At the time of her retirement in 1999 from the University of California, Los Angeles, Paula was professor of English, Creative Writing, and American Indian Studies. Among the awards she received were fellowships from the National Endowment for the Arts and the Ford Foundation-National Research Council; Hubbel Medal for Lifetime Achievement in American Literary Studies from the American Literature Division, Modern Language Association; a Lifetime Achievement Award from the Native Writers' Circle of the Americas; the Susan Koppelman Award from the Popular and American Culture Association; the Native American Prize for Literature; and a Lannan Foundation Fellowship awarded the year before her death.

Paula and I first met at the 1977 Summer Seminar on Contemporary Native American Literature, sponsored by the Modern Language Association and the National Endowment for the Humanities. Paula directed the seminar, which was held at Northern Arizona University, Flagstaff. Her humor and informality were crucial to the success of the seminar. For two weeks Native scholars and writers directed our discussions of works by American Indian writers. We attempted to define just what characterized Native American literature. During this heady time, many of us established life-long friendships. Paula used to laugh at and quote my reference to the group as the "Flagstaff Mafia."

The seminar spurred the establishment of the field of American Indian literature. In December 1977, seminar participants and others interested in the field met at the MLA convention in Chicago to develop a Discussion Group in American Indian Literatures, which became the Division of American Indian Literatures; to revitalize the Association for Study of American Indian Literature; and to establish a newsletter, which Karl Kroeber edited. During this memorable convention, Paula and many other seminar participants stayed at my house, where we had a huge party during the convention.

Another result of that seminar was the publication of *Studies in American Indian Literature: Critical Essays and Course Designs* (1983), which Paula edited. Containing essays and course designs by members of the seminar, this important book was teachers' first real guide to the field. While I was preparing supper during one of her visits to my home, Paula said she wanted me to write the essay on the history of American Indian literatures and prepare a bibliography. I, of course, agreed, not realizing I was setting out on a new career.

The obituary for Paula, distributed by the Newsroom at the University of California, Los Angeles, and various biographies of her describe her significant contributions to the field of American Indian literatures. A poet, novelist, and critic, she was a significant voice in the development of Native literature and literary criticism. Paula was a splendid poet, whose works reveal her imaginative observations, incisive insights, and mastery of poetic form. I think she was happiest creating poetry.

The Sacred Hoop: Recovering the Feminine in American Indian Traditions (1986), based on her doctoral dissertation, is one of the most widely cited works in the field. Paula's analysis of the roles of women in Native society and writing and her emphasis on the power of oral tradition in American Indian cultures were especially influential. She also expanded our knowledge of American Indian literatures through her editions of works by Native authors. Her last critical book, *Pocahontas: Medicine Woman, Spy, Entrepreneur, Diplomat* (2003), defiantly examines the life of Pocahontas from a Native perspective. Throughout her creative and critical writing, Paula stressed the significance of woman power. Her *America the Beautiful: The Final Poems of Paula Gunn Allen* is a poignant tribute to the land and people she loved. Patricia Clark Smith and John Crawford, close friends, carefully edited the manuscript, which was published posthumously by West End Press in 2010. The volume is a memorable last testament to Paula.

She and I became close friends after the Contemporary Native American Literature seminar. Because none of the seminar members really had colleagues in their departments interested in or knowledgeable about American Indian literatures, seminar participants frequently telephoned each other—no e-mail then. Paula and I talked often about our frustrations and occasional triumphs as we deepened our scholarship in the field or developed programs. We also got together during her book tours, when I could arrange readings for her at the University of Illinois, Chicago, or at Newberry Library. She always loved coming to Chicago—if the weather was warm.

During my visit to Albuquerque in the early 1980s, Paula and I had

brunch with her parents at their apartment so that we could see the
launching of the balloons during the annual race. Her parents and
one of her sisters treated me to a bountiful and delicious brunch. It
was a delight to be with her family and hear their stories and laughter. The visit was especially magical as we watched all the multi-
colored balloons gracefully rising in the air. Paula also took me to
visit her grandmother, a very kind lady who immediately welcomed
us to her home. Paula liked to talk about the joke she pulled on
Joseph Bruchac (Abenaki) during his visit to Albuquerque. She
asked him if he would like to see some ancient relics. After he excit-
edly said "Yes!", she took him to visit her parents and grandmother.
During my visit, we drove around the Laguna Reservation and
nearby villages to see the places where Paula grew up and which she
and Leslie Silko (Laguna) mentioned in their work.

In the summer of 1983, both Paula and Carol Lee Sanchez, her
older sister, were speakers at the University of Illinois, Chicago.
Carol Lee, who stayed at my house, was a speaker for a UIC-NEH
seminar on "Minority Women in the United States," or some such
title. Paula, who was a speaker in my NEH Summer Seminar on
American Indian Literature, also stayed with me. It was wonderful to have them together and to hear family stories and history.

During the three decades of our friendship, we have shared with
each other both our triumphs and our tragedies. Paula's fragile
health from chronic Epstein Barr Syndrome severely drained her
energy, as did a serious accident. Perhaps the hardest times for us
both were the deaths of our children. Paula's son, Eugene, died from
a fatal heart attack in October 2001 and my daughter, Sharon, died
of AIDS in January 2002. Paula never recovered from Eugene's
death. She had moved to Fort Bragg to be near him and her grandchildren, so that he could help her as she became increasingly frail.
Her grief after the crib death of Fuad never left her and Eugene's

death was almost too much. As mothers, we expect that we will grow older and eventually pass on, but we do not expect our children to die before us. When a child dies, one feels a profound sense of loss and imbalance. Paula and I often talked about this and usually called one another around the anniversaries of the deaths of our children. She was very grateful to her surviving children, Lauralee Brown Hannes and Suleiman Allen, for caring for her during her final illness.

Two of her last visits to Chicago occurred after the publication of her book on Pocahontas, when she performed stories and gave a reading at Newberry Library. By that time, Paula was so weak that she had to lie down before she was able to go on stage for her storytelling performance. Paula continued to write poetry and even took a poetry class at a local community college. Poetry was her great love and represented some of her very best writing. She was also a gifted storyteller. Paula told me fascinating stories about growing up in Cubero and about her experiences as a child. During her last two years. I urged her to write some children's books, because she was then too ill to attempt longer works. After a fire burned down her manufactured home and her car, she was later hospitalized for smoke inhalation as well as for lung cancer. Released from the hospital, she began sending to her friends "The Perils of Being Paula," three tragic and funny e-mail accounts of her experiences.

What I remember so vividly about Paula is her laughter and affection. No matter how sick she was, we would always burst into laughter during our phone conversations. Paula often said she liked to call me when she was depressed because what she described as "my wild sense of humor" made her feel better. Even when she telephoned to tell me she was dying, our conversation turned to storytelling and the ironies of life that made us both laugh. "Wouldn't you know," she said. "I've waited my whole life for a person of color to be elected president. When it finally might happen, I won't be here to see it."

The following excerpt from "Riding the Thunder" (1969) beautifully expresses her imagination and the power of her poetry:

> Climb the spruce tree and dance on tip
> Climb into the mountain when it opens for you
> Follow the winding corridors of shape and time
> Enter into the moving paths of shape and time
> On an eight-legged horse of blue flame arise,
> They will not send you back. (*Life is a Fatal Disease: Collected Poems, 1962-1995*, Albuquerque: West End, 1997, 99.)

Now free from pain, Paula has arisen on that horse of blue flame and entered into "the moving paths of shape and time." Farewell, treasured friend.

~\!/~

Dr. Mary Churchill, a long-time friend and former graduate student of Paula's, maintains a memorial website under the direction of Paula's family at http://www.paulagunnallen.net. The site is for the family, friends, colleagues, and admirers of Paula Gunn Allen, Ph.D., American Indian scholar and poet.

A Review of
America The Beautiful: Last Poems
by Paula Gunn Allen, West End Press, 2010

A. LaVonne Brown Ruoff

For three decades, Paula Gunn Allen was one of the most important voices in Native American literature and criticism. Her posthumous *America the Beautiful* is an eloquent and poignant tribute to the land and people she loved. In Part I, "America the Beautiful," Allen not only describes the beauty and power of nature, but she also fiercely warns of the danger it faces. Several of the poems are plays on words, which demonstrate Allen's love of language. In Part II, "There Is Another Shore," named for one of her most moving selections, she includes several personal poems on such topics as her own hubris, seeing herself as a bridge for others, and the excruciating pain of losing two sons. A forceful and touching book, *America the Beautiful* reminds us of what is important in the world and life. John Crawford and Patricia Clark Smith carefully organized and edited the book, for which Smith provided a charming introduction.

CONTRIBUTOR BIOGRAPHIES

Anasazi Rooms
Kristina Bitsue

CONTRIBUTOR BIOGRAPHIES

∻ **Márgara Averbach** is Doctora en Literatura (University of Buenos Aires) and Literary Translator (IES in Lenguas Vivas). She teaches Literature of the USA at the University of Buenos Aires and Literary Translation at the IES. She has translated more than 60 novels, published 7 Academic books in Spain and Argentina on Black and Native USA Literature; and fiction books for children, young people and adults. She won the National Argentine Library Prize for the novel *Una cuadra* (2008); the First Prize for Children Short Stories, Madres de Plaza de Mayo (1992); the First Prize for Stories on Identity, Abuelas de Plaza de Mayo, (2001) and the Conosur Prize for Technical Translation, Union Latina (2007). She was awarded the Konex Diploma for Literature for Young Adults (2014). Two of her novels for young people and adults, *El año de la Vaca* (2004) and *El agua quieta* (2015) were awarded the ALIJA prize, the main award for youth and children literature in Argentina.

∻ **Kristina Bitsue** is a member of the Dine' (Navajo) Nation. She is Tabaḥaa (Water's Edge Clan) born for Maiideeshgiizhni (Coyote Pass Clan). Kristina is a graduate of Dine' College in Tsaile, AZ. She began writing poetry in her elementary years of education and has continued to write ever since.

∻ **Jennifer Browdy** is Associate Professor of Comparative Literature and Media Studies at Bard College at Simon's Rock. The

Founding Director of the Berkshire Festival of Women Writers and co-founder of Green Fire Writers' Workshop. Jennifer invites others to use writing as a pathway to individual, social and environmental health through her writing, teaching, workshops and author coaching. Her new memoir, *What I Forgot . . . And Why I Remembered: A Journey to Environmental Awareness and Activism Through Purposeful Memoir*, is accompanied by her writer's guide, *The Elemental Journey of Purposeful Memoir: A Writer's Companion*. Jennifer has written for *Yes! Magazine, Kosmos Journal*, and many academic journals and has edited three anthologies of global women's writing, including *Women Writing Resistance in Latin America and the Caribbean* (Beacon Press, 2017) and *African Women Writing Resistance* (University of Wisconsin Press, 2010).

⁛ **Joseph Bruchac III** was born in 1942 in Saratoga Springs, NY. He earned a Ph.D. at the Union Graduate School in 1975. His awards include an American Book Award from the Before Columbus Foundation in 1984, a Wordcraft Circle Writer of the Year award in 1998 and a Wordcraft Circle Storyteller of the Year award in 1998. For over thirty years Bruchac has been creating poetry, short stories, novels, anthologies and music that reflect his Abenaki Indian heritage and Native American traditions. He is the author of more than 120 books for children and adults. The bestselling *Keepers of the Earth: Native American Stories and Environmental Activities for Children* and others of his "Keepers" series, with its remarkable integration of science and folklore, continue to receive critical acclaim and to be used in classrooms throughout the country.

⁛ **Menoukha R. Case** is an Associate Professor of Interdisciplinary Studies at SUNY Empire State College Center for Distance Learning. She holds an MA in Women's Studies, an MA in creative writing, and a PhD in African Diaspora literature through the lens of Yoruba philosophy, from the University at Albany. She is privileged to teach with and from Stephanie Seller's *Native American Women's Studies: A Primer.* Her poem/book, *Tidal River Sediment*, is published by Main Street Rag. Her academic work has appeared in books (*Black Writers and the Left*, ed. Kristin Moriah, chapter; *50 Events that Shaped American Indian History: An Encyclopedia of the American Mosaic*, ed. Donna Martinez & Jennifer Williams Bordeaux, chapter with Rhianna Rogers "Haudenosaunee/Iroquois Influence on the U.S. Constitution, 1789") and journals such as *Callaloo*, *Critical Sense*, and the Writer's Institute Newsletter. Her artwork is in *Xtant* as well as *Fingernails Across a Chalkboard: A Literary and Artistic View of HIV/AIDS Affecting People of Color*, and on the covers of Randall Horton's *Lingua Franca of Ninth Street*, and Truth Thomas's *Bottle of Life*. Her late partner, Larry Matrious, was an Anishinaabe Ojibwe who deepened her learning about Native Americans that had begun with reading Paula Gunn Allen.

⁘ **Sandra Cox** grew up in eastern New Mexico, holds a Ph.D. from the University of Kansas and currently lives in southern Ohio, where she teaches at Shawnee State University and chases her corgi, Jazz, through the foothills of Appalachia. Dr. Cox has recently published an article on the craft and politics of Menominee poet Chrystos in *Interdisciplinary Literary Studies*. She also has forthcoming contributions to a collection entitled *Bodies and Culture* that analyzes Muskogee author Craig Womack's and Coeur d'Alene/Spokane author Sherman Alexie's depictions of Native adolescent homoerotic desires in a collection entitled *Bodies and Culture*, and to the edited volume *Louise Erdrich: Critical Perspectives* on the invocations of Two-Spiritism in *The Beet Queen*.

⁘ **Carolyn Dunn** is an American Indian artist of Cherokee, Muskogee Creek, and Seminole descent on her father's side, and is Cajun, French Creole, and Tunica-Biloxi on her mother's. Her work has been recognized by the Wordcraft Circle of Storytellers and

Writers as Book of the Year for poetry (*Outfoxing Coyote*, 2002) as well as the Year's Best in 1999 for her short story "Salmon Creek Road Kill," Native American Music Awards (for the Mankillers CD *Comin to Getcha*) and the Humboldt Area Foundation. Additional books include *Through the Eye of the Deer* (Aunt Lute Books, 1999), *Hozho: Walking in Beauty* (McGraw Hill, 2002), *Coyote Speaks* (H.N. Abrams, 2008), *Echolocation: Poems, Stories and Songs from Indian Country: L.A.* (Fezziweg Press, 2013), and the forthcoming *The Stains of Burden and Dumb Luck* (Mongrel Empire Press, 2016).

❖ **Janice Gould**'s tribal affiliation is Concow/Maidu. She served as the Pike's Peak Poet Laureate from 2014-2016. Her latest collection, *The Force of Gratitude*, was a Finalist for the 2016 Charlotte Mew Chapbook Contest. Other collections of poetry include *Doubters and Dreamers*, *Earthquake Weather*, *Beneath My Heart*; two letter-pressed art books, *Alphabet* and *Indian Mascot, 1959*; and a co-edited collection of essays, *Speak to Me Words: Essays on Contemporary American Indian Poetry*. Janice is an Associate Professor in Women's and Ethnic Studies at the University of Colorado, Colorado Springs, where she teaches classes in Native American Studies.

❖ **LeAnne Howe,** Eidson Distinguished Professor at the University of Georgia, connects literature, Indigenous knowledge, Native histories, and expressive cultures in her work. Her interests include performance studies, film, and Indigeneity. Professor Howe (Choctaw) is the recipient of a United States Artists (USA) Ford Fellow, Lifetime Achievement Award by the Native Writers' Circle of the Americas, American Book Award, Oklahoma Book Award, and she was a Fulbright Distinguished Scholar to Jordan. Recently in October 2015, Howe received the Distinguished Achievement Award from the Western Literature Association,

(WLA); and in 2014 she received the Modern Languages Association inaugural Prize for Studies in Native American Literatures, Cultures, and Languages for Choctalking on Other Realities. Her books include, *Shell Shaker*, 2001, *Evidence of Red*, 2005, *Miko Kings: An Indian Baseball Story*, 2007, *Choctalking on Other Realities*, 2013. She co-edited a book of essays on Native films with Harvey Markowitz, and Denise K. Cummings titled, *Seeing Red, Pixeled Skins: American Indians and Film*, 2013.

∹ **Elaine Jacobs** ["EeeJay" to PGA] considers those first seven years with Paula and The Rainbow Warriors the best education she could have had and she will be eternally grateful. Elaine has worked in recording studios, computer R&D labs, (built a computer on-board the Hubble Space Telescope), theaters, and on lots of houses, including the Warriors' school in Paula's back yard, with the able help of many classmates. Her inner Fourth Way Work remains the deepest ongoing spiritual legacy of Dr. Gunn Allen's incomparable teachings.

∹ **Maurice Kenny** (1929-2016) A beloved and cantankerous poet of Mohawk and Seneca descent, Kenny made his literary mark during the Native American Literary Renaissance, particularly his Two-Spirit works, which are now considered pioneering works in the field. By the 1980s, Kenny's reputation as an author had been firmly established by such publications as *Blackrobe: Isaac Jogues* (1982) and *Between Two Rivers* (1987), both of which were nominated for the Pulitzer Prize, and *The Mama Poems* (1984), which won the American Book Award. He considered his 1992 book *Tekonwatonti: Molly Brant (1735-1795): Poems of War* to be his most important work. Kenny co-edited the influential *Contact/II* literary journal and ran the independent Strawberry Press, which focused primarily on publishing work by Native American authors. In the last weeks of his life, he shared with Stephanie that death, he feared, would soon stop for him, but meanwhile "the sun is bright and the dandelions will soon pop."

❖ **Barbara Alice Mann** is a full Professor of Humanities in the Jesup Scott Honors College, University of Toledo, Ohio. Author of thirteen books (and counting), along with over two hundred chapters and articles (still counting), she specializes in Native North American history and culture of the eighteenth and nineteenth centuries. Her secondary focuses are in Women's Studies and early nineteenth-century Literature. Her most recent books are *Spirits of Blood, Spirits of Breath: The Twinned Cosmos of Indigenous America* (Oxford, 2016) and *The Cooper Connection: The Influence of Jane Austen on James Fenimore Cooper* (AMS, 2014). Mann is co-chair of the Native American Alliance of Ohio.

❖ **Deborah A. Miranda** is an enrolled member of the Ohlone-Costanoan Esselen Nation of the Greater Monterey Bay Area in California. Her book *Bad Indians: A Tribal Memoir*, received the prestigious PEN-Oakland Josephine Miles Literary Award, a Gold Medal from the Independent Publishers Association, and was short-listed for the William Saroyan Literary Award. This book, now taught in hundreds of universities around the world, traces her family into, through, and out of the Carmel Mission from 1770-2013 with oral stories, mission records, family photographs, newspaper records, ethnographic field notes, and more. The author of three poetry collections—*Indian Cartography*, which won the Diane Decorah Award for First Book from the Native Writer's Circle of the Americas, *The Zen of La Llorona*, nominated for the Lambda Literary Award, and *Raised by Humans*—she is also working on a collection of essays, *The Hidden Stories of Isabel Meadows and Other California Indian Lacunae*, under contract with the University of Nebraska Press. A collection of persona poems in the voices of the 21 California missions, which includes her photographs and artwork, is in-progress. As a scholar, Deborah's research focuses on the lives of California Indians during and after missionization, Indigenous women's love poetry and erotics, and Two-spirit literature. Miranda is John Lucian Smith Jr. Endowed Chair of English at Washington and Lee University in Lexington, Virginia where she teaches creative writing and literature of the margins.

⁚ **A. LaVonne Brown Ruoff** is Professor Emerita of English at the University of Illinois, Chicago. She has received life-time scholarly achievement awards from the Modern Language Association and the American Book Award/Before Columbus Foundation. The director of four National Endowment for the Humanities Summer Seminars for College Teachers on American Indian Literature, Ruoff is the former general editor of the University of Nebraska Press's American Indian Lives Series. Her publications include *American Indian Literatures* (1990) and critical editions of works by Native authors George Copway, S. Alice Callahan, E. Pauline Johnson, and Charles Eastman.

⁚ **Stephanie A. Sellers** holds a doctoral degree in Native American Studies and teaches at Gettysburg College where she was awarded the 2013 Faculty Award for Community-based Engagement. Her most recent book is *Native American Women's Studies Primer* (Peter Lang 2008), which followed the publication of her doctoral dissertation titled *Native American Autobiography Redefined: A Handbook* (Peter Lang 2006). Her scholarship, poetry, essays, and coyote stories have been published in *The Routledge Companion to Native American Literature, Native Literatures: Generations, American Indian Culture & Research Journal*, and *Calyx: The Journal of Women's Literature and Art*, among others. She has lectured at the Elizabeth A. Sackler Center for Feminist Art at the Brooklyn Museum in NYC and at many other national conferences. Sellers is a homesteader with her husband Robert and their beloved Welsh Corgi in the mountains of Pennsylvania, and has a lifelong love of tilling the soil and gathering plant medicines. One of her favorite flowers is the fragrant, miniature jonquil 'Golden Echo.'

❧ **Patricia (Pat) Clark Smith** (12/14/1943–7/11/2010) attended Smith College as a scholarship student, graduating with a B.A. in 1964, and Yale University from 1964 to 1970, when she was awarded a Ph.D. in English. She taught English at University of New Mexico for thirty-two years, from 1971 to 2003. Early in her career at UNM she also taught at schools connected to several Navajo Indian reservations (Ramah and Sinosti) in New Mexico with pioneering New Mexico early childhood teacher Lenore Wolfe. Pat married teacher and small press publisher (West End Press) John Crawford in 1987. She is the Grandmother of Native American Women's Studies. One of her early Ph.D. students, Laguna Pueblo author Paula Gunn Allen, published a revised version of her doctoral dissertation as *The Sacred Hoop*, a groundbreaking approach to feminist studies in Native American literature, in 1986. Among Patricia's companions throughout this period were Native American writers Joy Harjo, Leslie Marmon Silko, Simon Ortiz and Luci Tapahonso. She published the first book of her own poems, *Talking to the Land*, in 1979. For other works, please see the dedication.

❧ **Lisa Tatonetti** is a Professor of English at Kansas State University where she studies, teaches, and publishes on queer Indigenous literatures. She is co-editor of *Sovereign Erotics*, an award-winning collection of Two-Spirit creative work, and author of *The Queerness of Native American Literature*, which won the 2015 Thomas J. Lyons Book Award and was selected for the ALA 2016 Over the Rainbow Recommended Reading List. Her current project "Big

Moms and Butch Dykes" considers female, Two-Spirit, and trans masculinities in Indigenous literatures.

: **Annette Van Dyke** is professor Emerita of English and Inter-disciplinary Studies at the University of Illinois Springfield. She has published numerous articles on the works of Paula Gunn Allen, Leslie Marmon Silko, Louise Erdrich, and Linda Hogan. She has retired to a floating home on the Willamette River in Oregon and is working on a memoir.

: **Gabrielle Welford** was born in the southwest of England and lived there for three weeks before sailing to India. She has been traveling and exploring the world since and, immersed in the sounds of other languages, finds words delicious. She has two children, Annie and Tolemy, and a Ph.D. ensured in good part by having Paula as a floating member on the dissertation committee. Annie was born at the end of a three-year constant engagement between a group of women and Paula Gunn Allen in Berkeley, California, in the mid-1980s. The relationship began as a work-shop in women's spirituality but quickly grew until we were meet-ing at Paula's house and at Mama Bear's café in Oakland several times a week. I know for certain that I would not have been able to decide to have my children and to be even as decent a mother as I was if it hadn't been for Paula and those gatherings.

WORKS CITED

ANNETTE VAN DYKE

Allen, Paula Gunn. "Beloved Women," *Conditions : Seven, A Magazine of Writing by Women with an Emphasis on Writing by Lesbians* III: 1 (Spring 1981): 65-87. Print.

———, "Judy Grahn: 'Gathering of the Tribe." *Contact II.* Special Issue on Women Poets. 5: 27-9(1982-83): 7-9. Print.

Bruchac, Joseph. Interview. "I Climb the Mesas in My Dreams." *Survival This Way: Interviews with American Indian Poets.* Tucson: U of Arizona P, 1987. 1-21. Print.

Eysturoy, Annie O. Interview. "Paula Gunn Allen." *This is About Vision: Interviews with Southwestern Writers.* Eds. William Balassi, John F. Crawford, and Anne O. Eysturoy. Albuquerque: U. of New Mexico P, 1990. Print.

Van Dyke, Annette. "A Tribute to Paula Gunn Allen." *Studies in American Indian Literatures* 20:4 (Winter 2008): 68-75. Print.

JENNIFER BROWDY

Gunn Allen, Paula. "The Perils of Being—3" http://www.greenmac.com/Paula/perils3.html, accessed June 30, 2009.

Allen, Paula Gunn. *The Sacred Hoop: Recovering the Feminine in American Indian Traditions.* Boston: Beacon Press, 1986. Print.

———. *Grandmothers of the Light: A Medicine Woman's Sourcebook.* Boston: Beacon, 1991.

Anzaldua, Gloria. *Interviews/Entrevistas.* Ed. AnaLouise Keating. NY: Routledge, 2000. Print.

SANDRA COX

Allen, Paula Gunn. *America the Beautiful: Last Poems*. Albuquerque, NM: West End Press, 2010. Print.

———. *The Sacred Hoop: Recovering the Feminine in American Indian Traditions*. Boston: Beacon Press, 1986. Print.

Berlant, Lauren and Elizabeth Freeman. "Queer Nationality." *Boundary*. 19.1 (1992) 149-80.

Brant, Beth. "Giveaway: Native Lesbian Writers." *Signs*. 18.4 (1993): 944-47. Print.

Cook-Lynn, Elizabeth. "The American Indian Fiction Writers: Cosmopolitanism, Nationalism, the Third World and First Nation Sovereignty." Eds. John Purdy and James Ruppert, *Nothing But the Truth: An Anthology of Native American Literature*. New Jersey: Prentice Hall, 2001. 23-38. Print.

———. "American Indian Intellectualism and the New Indian Story." *American Indian Quarterly*. 20:1 (1996) 57-76. Print.

Cox, James H. "Toward a Native American Critical Theory." *American Indian Quarterly*. 29:1 (2005) 316-21. Print.

Driskill, Qwo-Li. "Call Me Brother: Two-spiritness, the Erotic, and Mixed-blood Identity as Sites of Sovereignty and Resistance in Gregory Scofield's Poetry." Eds. Dean Rader and Janice Gould, *Speak to Me Words: Essays on Contemporary American Indian Poetry*. Tucson: Arizona UP, 2003. 222-34. Print.

———. "Stolen From Our Bodies: First Nations Two-Spirits/Queers and the Journey to a Sovereign Erotic." *Studies in American Indian Literatures*. 16.2 (2004). 50-62. Print.

Gamson, Joshua. "Must Identity Movements Self-Destruct? A Queer Dilemma." *Social Problems*. 42, 3. (1995): 390-407. Print.

Jacobs, Sue-Ellen, and Wesley Thomas and Sabine Lang. Eds. *Two-Spirit People: Native American Gender Identity, Sexuality and Spirituality*. Urbana-Champaign: U of Illinois, 1997. Print.

Lawrence, Bonita. "Gender, Race, and the Regulation of Native Identity in Canada and the United States: An Overview." *Hypatia*. 18.2 (2003) 3-31. Print.

Nagel, Joane. "Ethnicity and Sexuality." *Annual Review of Sociology*. 26. (2000). 107-33. Print.

Osborne, Karen. "Swimming Upstream: Recovering the Lesbian in Native American Literature." Ed. William Spurlin. *Lesbian and Gay Studies and the Teaching of English: Positions, Pedagogies and Cultural Politics*. Urbana, Illinois: National Council of Teachers of English, 2000. 191-210. Print.

Rader, Dean. "Word as Weapon: Visual Culture and Contemporary Indian Poetry." *MELUS*. 27.3 (2002) 147-68. Print.

Roscoe, Will, Ed. *Living the Spirit: A Gay American Indian Anthology*. New York: St. Martin's, 1988. Print.

Silko, Leslie Marmon. "Language and Literature from a Pueblo Indian Perspective." Eds. John Purdy and James Ruppert, *Nothing But the Truth: An Anthology of Native American Literature*. New Jersey: Prentice Hall, 2001. 160-66. Print.

Womack, Craig. "Politicizing HIV Prevention in Indian Country." Ed. Jace Weaver. *Native American Religious Identity: Unforgotten Gods*. New York: Orbis, 1998. 199-216. Print.

———. *Red on Red: Native American Literary Separatism*. Arizona UP: Tucson, 2001. Print.

A. LAVONNE BROWN RUOFF

Aal, Kathryn Machan. "Writing as an Indian Woman: An Interview with Paula Gunn Allen." *North Dakota Quarterly* 57 (1989):148-61. Print.